NAMING THE BODY:
A Queer Woman's Restorative Mapping of the Self

NAMING THE BODY

A Queer Woman's Restorative Mapping of the Self

MARÍA MÍNGUEZ ARIAS

Translated by Robin Myers

Naming the Body: A Queer Woman's Restorative Mapping of the Self

Mouthfeel Press is an indie press. We publish poetry, fiction, and nonfiction in English and Spanish by new and established poets and writers.

Cover Design: Cloud Cardona
Interior Design: Sadie Lynn Phelps
Cover Art: The Met open source

ISBN: 978-1-957840-50-5
Library of Congress Control Number: 2025949950
Published in the United States, 2026
First Printing in English $18

CONTENTS

My body and your bodies make a map we can follow... What our bodies, my mother's and yours and mine, require in order to thrive, is what the world requires. If there is a map to get there, it can be found in the atlas of our skin and bone and blood, in the tracks of neurotransmitters and antibodies. We need nourishment, equilibrium, water, connection, justice.

~Aurora Levins Morales, *Kindling: Writings on the Body*

Maps are tools for the struggle... They make injustices visible and are a powerful resource for political connection.

~Florencia Goldsman, *Píkara Magazine*

FOR

All women and those who love them

My rebellious body on its fiftieth birthday —

thank you for sustaining me

AND FOR

Rosie, always

NAMING THE BODY:

A Queer Woman's Restorative Mapping of the Self

THE LINE OF THE FLOOR

I'm lying on the floor in the short, narrow hallway of my house, which is teeming with firefighters. I can't see them, but I can hear them. I know they're firefighters because my partner called 911 and I heard the sirens approach until they filled the kitchen. When you make an emergency call like that, it's always the firefighters who show up first, and lots of them, a whole group. One of them speaks with the hospital, explains that they won't be able to move me until they find a pulse.

"What's your name?"

Another kneels by my head, so his voice reaches me from close range. I want to turn and look at him, but my neck won't react. I open my mouth to answer; the words won't leave. I lift my right hand as best I can, although my wrist doesn't follow suit, and the gesture is limited to a flutter of slow, useless fingers. I want to tell him that my name is María.

"Do you remember what your name is?"

I wriggle my fingers in the air again, my name hunched in the cavern of my throat. I don't know what else to do. I try to raise my hand again. This time my wrist obeys and my hand rises briefly before dropping back down in defeat. I feel as if my silence were stretching out time, tugging on the elastic as everyone waits.

"Maaaría," I manage to say at last, my voice somehow both frail and heavy. The problem isn't that I don't remember, I want to say, but that the words refuse to unhitch themselves from my throat.

"What's your birthday?"

"Juuuuune fiiiiifth niiiineteeeeen seeeveeeentyyyy."

"And your address?"

"I remeeeember eeeeverythiiiing," I tell him. "Thiiiis… this has happened to me before."

The syllables peer out from behind my teeth. Time's rubber keeps stretching.

"Iiiit woooon't laaast loooong."

"She has a three-inch laceration on her forehead." The other fireman is still talking with the hospital.

Three inches? I do some quick calculations: six, seven centimeters? I don't want to even try to picture my forehead right now. Although I'm more worried about my foot, which is incredibly painful. I fear it's broken. And my legs are cold, I'm freezing. I prod my right leg with sluggish fingers and realize I'm not wearing any pants. That's when I remember I'm in my underwear. That's when I remember that the doorbell rang and I dashed toward the bedroom so that our guests wouldn't find me half-naked. And now, life — that joker with a sick sense of humor who hates it when you get too comfortable in the day-to-day — has me sprawled out like this, in my own hallway, in my underwear, surrounded by the entire squad of Fire Station #1! A whole battalion of burly men, I sense, rectangular as doors, because whenever one of them moves, the floor trembles under my back.

It's a Saturday afternoon. A few hours earlier, we decide we'd better take a nap, because we have two little kids between the ages of two and five and we've got family coming over soon; we're celebrating. If we don't want one kid throwing a tantrum and the other leaping around like the Energizer Bunny, they'd better sleep for a bit. Ignoring what we already know, which is that naps are fleeting in this house, especially family naps, all four of us get into our bed. For some reason we felt like nesting with our kittens today. We separate the little ones, because the girl needs space to sleep and the boy needs to toss and turn a gazillion times. Soon we're beside ourselves: the girl because the boy won't stop fidgeting, the boy because he has to move and doesn't have enough room, and the moms because we have to shield our faces every time the boy shifts in bed so he won't head-butt us and chip one of our teeth, which wouldn't be the first time — and because, truth be told, good grief, we just don't fit in the damn bed. After a while, I get up and carry the boy to his room, which is what we should have done to begin with. He's two, and he struggles mightily to fall asleep, as do I to get him there. A year later, he'll have a revelation: he'll jump out of bed, shoot into the living room, and exclaim in Spanglish, "I don't fall asleep porque tengo mucha energía que usar!" There's a pretty simple ritual: if I want him to nap, I have to lie down next to him and wait the twenty or thirty minutes it takes for him to "use his energy," even though what he actually does is get rid of it, burn it, consume it, exhaust it. So I lie down by his side. He's even more wound-up than usual this afternoon, as if he could tell I need him to sleep; half an hour later, he's still turning somersaults. By the time he succumbs to slumber, it's been an hour, I'm sweaty and exhausted, and I no longer want to spend another minute with my adorable family. I pull off my jeans, grab a blanket, and retreat to the sofa for the kind of nap decreed by the goddesses: alone, spread out.

I don't know how long I've been zonked when the doorbell rings. I sit bolt upright and glance around. I'm disoriented, uprooted from a deep sleep. There's a loud knocking at the door, just a few yards from the sofa. I think I can make out the voice of my sister-in-law, the oldest, who has just driven over two hours to spend some time with us. I spring to my feet and lurch toward our bedroom in search of some pants. My left foot catches between the blanket and the sofa leg and I crash headfirst into a corner of the hall: the edge that juts out of our L-shaped corridor, and which I personally reinforced with aluminum molding under the plaster so that the nicks and collisions wouldn't eat away at it. And so, thanks to the impenetrable aluminum molding, I eat the corner myself, devour it whole. My partner will later say it felt like being jolted by an earthquake — but since it stopped, she fell right back asleep. That's Californians for you: they're rarely ruffled by a little tremor. It took her several minutes to realize that the earthquake was me.

The crash halts all my functions: all but the neurotransmitters responsible for pain. I'm not aware of having a torso, arms, or legs, not even a head; all I know is that I exist in an enormous ball of pain I can locate in the upper part of what was supposed to be my body. I hear voices beyond the door, and I want to yell for them to give me a minute, but I have no voice, because I have nothing, am nothing, only pain. Like an animal struck by a car, I want to crawl on all fours toward our bedroom and tell my partner to get the door. I lift my right arm to take that first step, but it's insanely heavy; I can't raise it from the ground. I can't see, either; I drag myself along the hall I've memorized, as if the hands and feet supporting me were four colossal magnets and the wood under my limbs were an iron beam. Time doesn't exist on this long journey; I know it's long because it has no end. When I think I've reached the bedroom door, I raise my right arm to knock, but all I can do is touch the wood before my hand slides down again, unable to strike. That's when the door swings open and I see my partner's bare feet. I try with all my strength to lift my head and tell her to answer the door, that I've taken quite a spill. Just as my eyes settle on my partner's knees, something hot and delicate trickles down the curve of my nose, the corner of my lips, my neck. I don't see the drops of blood on the wood floor until my head droops low again, wearied by my efforts.

Over the next few minutes, I begin to recover from the concussion I won't learn for several years that I even had. I'm increasingly conscious of where I am, what's going on around me. I figure out from the conversations in the hallway that the ambulance has arrived. I have a body now. I repeat to them that I feel a terrible pain in my foot, that I can't move it, but they're still fixated on my pulse, insisting that they can't move me until it stabilizes. I'm all too familiar with this fleeting pulse. I want to tell them not to worry, it'll be back, it has always come back.

Sometimes my life escapes from my body and I have to lie down.

My first fainting spell, like every memorable biographical landmark, has a date and a place: August 1982, in Mazatlán, Mexico. I'm twelve years old. It occurs on our second road trip around North America. The first, two years prior, took us around the northwestern United States and Canada; this time, in the summer of '82, we drive through the southwestern United States and Mexico. We've reached the coast the day before. I remember being with my brother and sister, I think in the hotel pool, and starting to feel strange, a discomfort I've never experienced until then, as if something inside me weren't working properly. I leave my siblings and go looking for my parents. It must be evening, because my father's already at the bar, and I make my way there via the little shortcut to the beach. He and the bartender are chatting and laughing. I ask for my mother; he says she went down to the water. I follow the path toward the sand, where I find her in conversation with a woman selling cloth dolls. I sit down on a beach chair and wait for a pause so I can explain what's happening to me, but their sentences click into place one after the other and I can't make my way in. I start to feel weakened by the strange sensation as it works on me from deep inside.

"Mamá," I interrupt at last.

"Yes, honey," she answers, not looking up from the doll in her hands.

"I don't feel well."

"What's wrong?" She looks at me.

"I don't know, I feel weird."

The woman keeps talking about the doll, my mother turns back to her and says something I can't decipher because everything reaches me sounding muffled, warped. I suspect that any dense, pasty time I've got left is running out, and I don't think I'll have the strength to elbow my way into the two women's chit-chat. I get up and go back to my father. As I follow the path up to the bar, I feel like I'm melting into the air.

"Papáaaaa," I shout faintly, "I caaaan't..."

My father's head peeks up from behind the foliage. I'm dissolving. My father runs toward me. The last thing I remember are his enormous hands gripping me under the armpits as I tip forward. When I come to, I'm lying on one of the tables at the bar and the barman, laughing, is making me the largest Shirley Temple I've ever seen in my life.

"That's what happens to tourists from up north, they drop like flies in this heat."

Thanks to the bartender's diagnosis (tourist with acclimatization deficit disorder), my fainting spell warrants no further attention until a year later, when, after a soccer game with some neighborhood kids under a punishing Castilian sun, I come home and keel over onto the floor as I leave the bathroom, right in front of my mother. This time my unconsciousness is accompanied by a seizure. And so begin the rounds of specialists and tests that never diagnose anything, but which at least reassure us that I don't have epilepsy, diabetes, or any of the other horrible things that surely scroll through my mother's mind, though she doesn't dare speak them aloud. Today, I'm amazed by my mother's stoicism; even in taking me to one specialist after another, she never conveyed a jot of danger or anxiety. When I become the mother of a young child with a debilitating chronic illness, I'll instinctively follow her example and adapt it to our circumstances. I'm even more astonished to remember the depth of her empathy on the mornings when I'd wake up and ask her to let me stay home from school because I felt weird — the only word I could find to explain what I felt, long before I came to understand what was happening inside — and she would, no questions asked. Other mothers, me included, would have sent their daughter to school for her inability to argue or explain herself.

Over the next few years, I come undone in the most unexpected places: hanging out with my friends from school one summer afternoon, when I find myself sitting on the curb because I can't stay upright anymore and, in a stroke of incredible luck, the only car driving down the deserted Avenida de Guadalajara is the town doctor, who notices my extreme pallor from the other side of the street and comes to my aid. At handball practice, my coach and the team representative carry chocolate bars with them: when I start to plummet, I leave the field, lie down on the ground, and eat chocolate until it passes, and I can return to my place at the goal post. When I'm finally old enough to drive and my little brother, who once went pale at the sight of too much blood, needs to go in for some lab work, I offer to go with him and explain the importance of not watching the extraction . . . but the person who ends up flat out on the floor of the clinic is me and not him.

For over two decades, in the absence of any clear diagnosis but suspecting that heat and fatigue have something to do with my symptoms, I learn to manage the uncertainty and shame I feel when I have to sit or lie down wherever and whenever the appearance of my symptoms demands it: the hallways of clinics and hospitals, badminton or soccer fields, supermarket aisles, the waiting room at the dentist, by the treadmill at the gym, certain July afternoons while vacationing in Spain without my partner, and my mother, sister, or sister-in-law have to take care of my children while I lie down on the nearest couch because I'm dissolving again.

On the evening when the firefighters refuse to transfer me out of the hallway until my pulse stabilizes, I'm a 37-year-old woman who has become perfectly acclimated to the line of the floor as the last resort against imminent unconsciousness. When my pulse finally appears, they move me onto a stretcher and carry me out to the ambulance, where the EMT greets me with a smile.

"How are you feeling?"

"I'm okay." And it's true: at least I can talk now, even if my words still drag.

"That took a while!"

"Yeah," I say, "they couldn't move me until they found my pulse."

"Vasovagal syncope can do that to you!" he says as he examines the gash on my forehead.

"What was that?" I ask, stunned — because it's possible that this guy has just diagnosed me.

"Vasovagal syncope," he repeats.

"Can you spell that for me, please?"

"V-a-s-o-v-a-g-a-l s-y-n-c-o-p-e."

Unable to move, lacking a phone or anything to write with, I memorize letter by letter the two words that will forever change my life.

Twenty-five years after the first time I fainted in Mazatlán, I finally know what's wrong with me! I say it, repeat it, spell it out, tell it to my partner, Google it, translate it, and call my mother, who jots it down. As soon as we hang up, I know she'll Google it too, in English and Spanish. But I wait a few months before fully familiarizing myself with the term and its consequences, because I still have a nasty foot sprain and an enormous seam across my forehead to look after.

> *Vasovagal syncope is a condition that leads to fainting when the body reacts to certain triggers, such as blood or intense emotions. It is also known as neurocardiogenic syncope. Vasovagal syncope causes a sudden drop in heart rate and blood pressure, which leads to diminished blood flow to the brain and causes a loss of consciousness. Vasovagal syncope is usually not harmful and does not require treatment. But fainting episodes can cause injuries due to falls and sudden blows.*

It turns out that what makes me spend so many hours of my life with my feet up is nothing but the threat of a blackout, a fit, a dizzy spell like those suffered by young ladies in *costumbrista* novels. My heart sinks at the mere thought that, had I been born a wealthy Spanish maiden in the eighteenth century, I would have become one of those spinsters who spend whole novels and movies crocheting in a corner because they're not good for much else. That's the image accompanied by the fainting fit, one that condemns its lady victim to fragility and helplessness. If I'd been born into the proletariat, I would have become one of those spinsters who spend whole novels and movies peeling potatoes by the stove because they're not good for much else. Although I do acknowledge that my spinsterhood would have had less to do with my dizzy spells than with my refusal to lie with a man for life.

In the third option, this one unrelated to my social class, I would have been committed to a convent. While interesting, at least it would have allowed me to write and even pursue intimate relationships with other cloistered women — this is an alternative I wouldn't have considered, because I'm an atheist; because I wouldn't have wanted to erect any more walls around myself than necessary; and because, most of all, I would have refused to lie with a man for life, no matter how mystical our union. I prefer to fantasize that, if I'd lived in the eighteenth century, I would have been born in Madrid and had a knack for sewing, and that I'd have shared a home in an old *corrala* house with my seamstress partner, a woman with whom I'd lie very pleasurably in the same bed — for life, why not. We would have brought our little ones from the village to the city — reincarnated as nieces and nephews, in our case — as so many other single women did at that time.

But I'll abandon the historical-biographical reverie of fainting fits in women who love other women and return to the joy I find in discovering both my diagnosis and the language that accompanies it: words like neuocardiogenic, autonomous nervous system, vagus nerve, blood pressure, memory loss, dizziness, vertigo, lethargy, drowsiness, loss of consciousness, weakness, changes of vision, restriction of the visual field, headaches…I decode the diagnosis and its vocabulary through internet searches and a bilingual glossary, as I've done and still do with our son's asthma attacks and bouts of pneumonia. I work hard to construct a solid scaffold of vasovagal syncope in both languages and devote myself to working on our shared history: past, present, and future.

It's extremely difficult to string together a story when you lack the language that connects the dots of the narrative. But now that I have my vocabulary, thanks to the EMT, all I have to do is go back in time and fill in the gaps with my diagnosis and its brand-new symptoms and meanings. The challenge of returning to the past, in hopes of implanting knowledge you acquired decades later and reconstructing a narrative, is that you invariably end up deep in the realm of speculation — and therefore of fiction.

So, more than returning to the past and trying to study it through the lens of diagnosis, I'd rather return to the past by posing a series of questions: What would have happened if all those teenage medical appointments had diagnosed me with vasovagal syncope then, despite all the uncertainties that this diagnosis entails? Would I still have been able to play soccer in the street until nightfall, as I actually had? Would I have played handball at the national level, as I eventually did? Would I have backpacked all over Europe with my friends without calling home along the way? Would I have had the freedom of movement my parents let me enjoy? Would I have driven the hundreds and hundreds of miles I drove all over Spain, alone at the wheel, as soon as I bought my first car? It didn't have air conditioning, so I drove with the windows down in the summer, pouring bottles of water onto myself to keep my body temperature down. Would I have worked at the warehouse, the call center, the electronics assembly floor? Would I have taken a chance on pregnancy and motherhood?

I'd venture to speculate that, even without being forced to inhabit an eighteenth-century novel, I may not have been able to travel solo in Spain or across Europe the way I did. I suppose I would have worked whatever job I'd found because I would have had no other choice. But I'm not sure, I'll confess, I would have hazarded motherhood. What I do know is that since my best years, vasovagally speaking, are from age twenty to nearly forty, and they coincide with my desire to be a mother, my pregnancy, and the early years of parenthood, we might say that my personal experience of motherhood was made possible by something of a miracle.

My diagnosis also equips me with certain tricks to plan ahead and protect me from fainting: more hours of sleep, electrolytes first thing in the morning after my coffee, a more careful management of my emotions, light meals with enough salt, an hour of rest on the couch just before I pick up my kids from school, a mid-afternoon coffee…and it works! Suddenly I find myself back at the gym, I start running again, I feel a bit less like I'm dragging my way through life. They're pretty good years: I join the board at my kids' cooperative preschool, I coordinate the support group for Latin American families at their elementary school; I translate and interpret for the families and teachers, organize a hiking group for kids; we camp across California, visit Spain, and explore the UK; I write my first novel. . . .

And yet the syncope, accustomed to navigating my attempts at a semi-normal life, surprises me once more. At some point it decides that my periods are abundant enough to destabilize my vagosympathetic balance: each period is followed by about ten days of tremendous instability, which manifests itself in the deceleration of my brain activity, plus a bodily debilitation so extreme that I have to recover on the couch from tasks as simple as a trip to the grocery story. I have to schedule any and all physical activity for the two weeks prior to my period; afterwards there's no way I can participate. For every hour out and about, every hour at the gym, I need two more to regain my strength.

It's the era of twofold grief. The first is for the loss of the life I'll no longer live. I'm forty-five years old and feeling more and more trapped by this volatility, both so familiar and so strange; the physical and mental restrictions are intensifying. The second grief is because I no longer experience my relationship with the syncope (now more a syndrome than anything else) as a challenge, but as a hostile confrontation in which negotiation and commitment just aren't cutting it anymore. The terms of our relationship change because I'm too young to feel so besieged, and my rebellion, as it has done so many other times, decides to take matters into its own hands. How, though? The only way it knows how: by learning as much as it can.

Since my syncope/syndrome and the health care system always shared a cagey bond, I decide I don't have time for more doctor's appointments or tests or postponements, and I get even more involved in studying my pathology and its *modus operandi.* That's how I reach the great epiphany of my forties: if I want to regain my balance on the tightrope that is vasovagal syncope, I must do away with my periods altogether.

Armed with information, I march in to see my OB-GYN and explain the terrible decline in my quality of life: I've been reduced to crawling along between ten days and two weeks per month, the circle of my every day is closing in on me, and all of this may have a very simple solution. We talk and hear each other out and come up with a plan: we'll start with a contraceptive, and if that doesn't work, we'll move on to an endometrial ablation. I don't have time for IUDs and I don't even want to think about a hysterectomy, as my body doesn't do well with post-op; the ablation sounds like it could be the midpoint I'm looking for.

On the day of my procedure, I step into the office of another OB-GYN specialized, I assume, in ablations. After we make our introductions, she asks if I'm willing to consider other less invasive, less physically risky options. I explain that I want to put an end to my periods as soon as possible, that I can't take it anymore, I'm drained and desperate, I don't know if I can bear to keep negotiating. I hold back tears. She talks, I listen, she convinces me. When I leave the clinic, I'm the bearer of an intrauterine device loaded with progestogen and hope and a five-year expiration date. I cross my fingers and lie down to see what happens.

And thus, almost without realizing, I begin a new relationship with my syncope: the phase of vagosympathetic equilibrium. For the first time in many years, I can look for work outside of the house because the veil of mental and physical restrictions seems to be lifting, because the person I am can offer herself to herself and to others, being present and available in a far more complex and enriching way. After a two-year search and numerous blows, I find the part-time job I've been hoping for; it needs to be part-time for the sake of availability to myself, to my writing, to other people. That's how I find myself at a small San Francisco publishing house that combines so many of my passions and obsessions. The city and neighborhood of its location are a return in their own right, because that's where my mother set out for Spain in the sixties, to settle down and have a family. And editorial curation is a way to gain literary ground for more women writers to inhabit — making room, most of all, for the work of queer, indigenous, and POC writers who have been excluded from the mainstream publishing industry. For the first time in my life, I'm working in a place where I can freely show and share of myself as the queer woman I am.

I can't possibly know what the future holds for the syndrome and me, how our story will continue, whether the vocabulary of our shared experience will expand or we'll stay as we are. If the pandemic has served any purpose at all, it has been to show this funambulist, inching her way along the vasovagal tightrope, that balance is by nature elusive, deceptive, fluctuating. And if she's going to maintain it, she'll need not only her own stubbornness, rebelliousness, and will, but also the support and empathy of her partner and children — always ready to take the reins of the everyday cart when life escapes the body of this companion and mother and she needs to lie down.

YOUR WORD AND MY BODY

I love you, cariño
She's so pretty
She has such big eyes
Qué bonita es
Look at those cheeks!
She's so quiet
Oh, come on, she already knows how to ride a bike
and she can't even reach the pedals!
She can't recite the poem,
poor thing, you can tell she doesn't
have it memorized
She never says a word, does she?
She talks too much
My daughter is free to talk whenever she wants
Look at her, such a young lady in that dress
Why won't she sing like the other girls?
She talks too much
If you'd just smile a little more
you'd be prettier
Hypocrite
I love you, honey

Come on, girl, smile,
it's like you don't even want to be in the picture
She's a dyke
Don't bother smiling,
dear
So what do they eat over there,
you've put on a few pounds
Dirty, filthy American pig
You should see the tomboy playing soccer!
Always talking back!
If she raises her voice, it's because she must have seen something
I love listening to you, tell me another story
She's horsey-looking
Her friend is the hot one
You always thought you were so smart!
Want to be my girlfriend?
I really like you
You're the best goalie in Castilla-La Mancha!
If you didn't want to mess around with me
you should have said so two hours ago
I'm very proud of you
She says she's almost positive you're a lesbian
I love you, kiddo
I love you, cielo
Why haven't I ever seen you with a guy?
Your hips are my favorite part of your body
and the line of your belly

You're a knockout
You're so thin, it's not normal,
especially for you
Are you sure you're eating?
I like you
So you had boyfriends too?
Her body's not bad, but her face
Has anybody ever told you how sexy you are!
If you're happy,
so am I
I love you
Lorca was like that,
then they killed him
Your belly is so small,
how far along did you say you were?
You're both such brave women!
So,
who's the father?
You're amazing, my love
Who's the guy in the relationship?
If you insist on a natural birth after
a C-section, sign here to exempt us
from all liability
I'm so proud of you, dear
You're brave
We need the father's signature!

Wait, I'm confused,
why is she here too?
You're both very strong, you've got this
You're incredible, hermana
Mamá, te quiero
I love you, Mamá
Your moms are disgusting!
You must have a father,
everybody has one
I like this button for you, Mamá:
"You are perfectly queer"
Mamá, you two are a power couple

FATHERLY TRINITY

The knuckles of my right hand grip his erection. Not me, not my hand, but the four small round bones peeking over the edge of the desk I lean against so I can overhear what the other girl is saying; my diminutive bony protuberances against his muscular one, swelling behind the corduroy of his pants. There are several of us sitting around the table, mostly girls and one boy, conspiring, I'm pretty sure, against the priest, our religion teacher, who keeps showing his face in this class despite the havoc we wreak in it. He's a nice man, cheerful, meek and easy to embarrass, slightly addled, who doesn't seem to understand that it's 1985 and we've outgrown religion class altogether. Franco has been dead and buried for a decade now, and the Spain I live in has just transitioned into democracy and plurality — or at least, that's what we're told, and we believe it. We live our lives between Madonna and Rosendo, between the club called Éxtasis and the bar called El Asturiano, between the school cafeteria and the wall that separates the campus from the vacant lot on the outskirts of town, where joints are passed from hand to hand, especially during religion class, when the priest expounds on Jesus to the empty chairs (the hooky-players will steal the truancy reports before they ever reach the vice principal's office) and otherwise absent attendants (who blow bubbles and snap their gum, popping mutedly in their mouths, and read *Súper Pop* under their desks).

I alternate between one kind of absence and the other. When I decide to stay put and keep my seat warm, I don't read *Súper Pop* but listen to the little old man speak from his dais and wonder when we'll finally break him; when he'll renounce, if not his God, then at least this gang of caustic, impossible 15-year-olds he's supposed to teach. Sometimes I pencil song titles onto my desk, then erase them, because in this year of high school (my second) they're constantly moving us around and we don't have our own desks. They separate us because they don't know how else to keep us in check. And we don't either, truth be told. Sometimes I wish I didn't have to live with this unease that keeps me from sitting still.

Furtively, I retract my hand, walk around the desk, and lean against the other side. In a few seconds, I feel the brush of the erect penis against my knuckles again. I know who it belongs to: I recognize him by his brown pants and the reek of sweat that radiates from his knit sweater. My classmate is a quiet boy, greasy-haired and speckled all over with acne. He's a nice guy, as the priest himself may very well have been; like the priest, too, he seems lost.

Use without the consent of the used is abuse, Audre Lorde wrote seven years prior. And even so, nothing in me rebels or even squirms; mostly what I feel is discomfort and pity for this confusing apprentice of adulthood. I don't say a word, don't even look at him, just get up and walk out of the classroom, bound for the wall where the truants gather.

Two years later, on a winter weekend, I visit Coimbra with a friend and her family. After a late, sumptuous lunch, she and I make our way to the boardwalk to take in the last rays of sun. Sitting on the wall that divides the boardwalk from the deserted beach below, we can't take our eyes from the water as we talk, captivated by the diligent murmur of the waves — which is why we don't see the only man on the beach, standing a few yards away, leaning against the wall. I see him first, when I sense a slight movement out of the corner of my eye and turn to look: the guy is masturbating as he stares at us. I don't see his genitals, though there's no need. I look away and stand up, projecting a calm I don't feel.

"Let's go," I tell my friend.

"What? Now? Why?" she asks, puzzled.

"There's a guy jacking off down there."

"Motherfucker!"

She doesn't even bother to look, just gets up too, and we carry on our way, change the subject, leave the beach, and soon forget about the guy.

The same friend and I emerge from a Scandinavian train station (in Copenhagen, or maybe Oslo) one morning in the summer of '89, backpacks in tow, map in hand. Whenever we can, we travel at night to save money on camping fees or youth hostels. It's early and we're still half-asleep. Since my friend hasn't yet put her contacts in, I'm the one who holds the map and tries to get her bearings so we can head toward the city center. I scrutinize the map in vain, can't figure out where we are. Nearby there's a parked car with the window down. I think I see someone at the wheel, but I'm not really looking; I'm not, or wasn't, the sort of person who easily strikes up conversation with strangers, not even to ask for directions. My friend quickly realizes that if we want to get out of there and make it downtown before lunch, we'll have to ask, so she grabs the map and approaches the car. I follow, because that's how we communicate: we both semi-speak English, and it's the sum of our fumbling that makes us more or less comprehensible. Same when we listen: we understand better together than apart. When she leans over to address the driver, I see the man's penis rising up from his open fly. I instantly suspect that we're being confronted with a bona fide act of *masturbari interruptus*: exposed penis, man gripping the wheel, both of us equally flustered. My friend holds the map in one hand, gesturing with the other to the grid of the old city, and asks. Still without her contacts, she can't see more than the guy's face.

"Let's go! Come on!" I say, pulling on her sleeve.

"What?" she says, not turning to look at me, extending the map to the man.

"He's not going to help us!" I yank her toward me harder.

"But I haven't even asked him!"

"He's got his dick out! Jesus Christ! Didn't you see it?"

"How can I see anything without my contacts. What an asshole!"

In the summer of '93, I'm interning as a journalist at the OTR/Press news agency in Madrid. I've just started and don't know anyone. On my lunch break, I go almost every day to the VIPs chain restaurant on Calle O'Donnell, get myself something to eat, and sit in Parque del Retiro to read. The heat is less punishing than usual for summer in Madrid. Sitting cross-legged in the shade of a tree with a book in my lap, I feel like a lucky girl. I don't remember which book, but I do recall experiencing one of those moments when you have to stop and let your brain savor what you've just read.

I look up to take in the temperate midday scene and appreciate the present, dignify it, and that's when I see him: propped up on his right elbow maybe ten yards away. He stares, his left hand rubbing his penis with a casual confidence that leaves me dumbfounded. The park is swarming with people at this hour. I look him in the eye, because I'm sitting down and don't know how to get up quickly and make a break for it without calling attention to myself, and also because at this point, well, at this point I want to know who the asshole is, as my friend would call him, who's jacking off this time. He even smiles, the son of a bitch. No one around me seems to notice. I lower my head and keep reading. After a minute, I close the book, get to my feet, and return to the office, taking great pains to avoid the eyes of my third public *homo masturbante* in five years.

Use without the consent of the used is abuse, Audre Lorde wrote fourteen years prior. And even so, there I am, I who never gave my consent of any kind, I who was never asked, bending over backwards to not make a scene, to not provoke, convincing myself that a guy masturbating right in plain view doesn't actually have anything to do with me and everything to do with his inability to get off on his own, his own lack of imagination, his own particular myopic view of pleasure and desire.

In 1997, I've just arrived at the Highland Hospital in the Bay Area, where I live. In the waiting room — a small expansion of the hallway with two rows of chairs, one right in front of the other — I see three people on one side and, on the other, a man who can't be over thirty, disheveled and soiled, slumped in his seat, his legs blocking the path. As I approach, a powerful stench of urine fills my nostrils; I fight the urge to cover my nose and hold my breath. When he sees me coming closer, he pulls in his long legs to let me pass. At the sight of his gentle eyes, I automatically decide to sit near him, in that section of the room, and keep him company, albeit from two seats down. He quickly strikes up a conversation, asking if I'd like to see a photo of his girlfriend. I smile and say I would. He sticks a hand into his pocket and extracts a Polaroid, leans over the seats that separate us, and presents it to me proudly.

"Isn't she pretty?"

I look. It's a photo of a woman's pussy. She's lying on a bed with her legs spread open and the image was taken from the level of her feet. From that angle, she's a faceless body.

"Isn't she pretty?" he insists, holding out the photo in front of me. The man has long fingers and surprisingly clean nails.

I try not to look at the girl's pussy and breasts, although they take up almost the entire frame. What would the headless woman think if she knew this guy was displaying her like a hunting trophy?

"Yes," I say, and wait for him to sit back in his seat, get up, and wind my way out.

Use without the consent of the used is abuse, Audre Lorde

wrote fourteen years prior. And even so, there I am again, nodding, granting my approval to the pussy of the faceless woman, getting up and taking the long way around the waiting room, hoping not to call attention to myself, not to spark some violent reaction from the guy, not to spark a violent reaction from any of the other patients, not to inadvertently get him kicked out of the hospital, no questions asked.

In vain, I spend my adolescence and youth outraged by the abuse of authority, the fallacy of indoctrination (political, religious, domestic), the manipulation and commercialization of the female body and its image. My struggle is always against the Fatherly Trinity that determines my every move: against the Father, the Son, and the Holy Spirit, and against the Pope, the Priest, the Bishop, the High School Principal, the Teacher, the Grandpa, the Uncle, the Brother, the Cousin, the Butcher, the Mayor, the Policeman, the Soldier, the Next-Door Neighbor, even the other neighbor two doors down; the rosary of men around whom my daily routine revolves. And nonetheless, my *homo masturbantes* don't spark any outrage in me at all. On the contrary, I pity them. What's more, it doesn't even cross my mind that the victim of such (dis-)encounters could be me. There's no rape, no one is forcing me to do anything I don't want to do except, perhaps, briefly, to look. What are these individuals taking advantage of, exactly? Is it possible to sexually abuse a body in public spaces without ever touching it?

Forty-two years after its publication, I finally read Audre Lorde's essay "Uses of the Erotic: The Erotic as Power," and

I'm floored to realize, for the first time in my life and with terrible clarity, that all of those incidents have everything to do with me and my own diminished power. That is, they're directly related to the abuse of authority I've been rebelling against since my teenage years. I'm horrified to learn that I didn't manage to feel outraged by any of these men because I grew up inhabiting a highly disciplined woman's body that occasionally disobeyed, but which generally, and predictably, abided by the established rules of conduct and decorum; a woman's body whose magnificent generative power I discover late in the game, because the disciplined body is ignorant of its true strength and capacity until it breaks the ties that have disciplined it. For me, it was my relationship with another woman, and the life project we shared, that embodied the beginning of the end of those tethers; the birth of our children disintegrated them once and for all. Today, I'd dare to say, I inhabit a woman's body that's far less disciplined and far more powerful than it was in her teenage years and twenties.

To Audre Lorde, everything is about power and who wields it: the more powerless you are, whether as a person or as a community, the easier it is to become a victim of abuse. Her essay explains that, in order to last, every act of oppression must dynamite the sources of power within the culture of the oppressed. For women, she believes, this has entailed the suppression of their eroticism as a source of power and regenerative information.

Lorde defends eroticism as an innate spiritual resource possessed by every woman; a resource directly associated with her emotions, feelings, and sensations. Lorde warns us that eroticism shouldn't be mistaken for pornography, as the latter entails the negation of the former in its suppression of emotion, feeling, and sensation: the coordinates of eroticism itself.

When a woman makes contact with her own eroticism — which is to say, when she acknowledges her emotions, feelings, and sensations, not only in sex, but in everything she does — and experiences the resulting satisfaction and fulfillment for the first time, she learns not to expect less of herself. Lorde relates how, in recognizing her own eroticism, she felt empowered to access her own knowledge and creative energy, which she then used to defend her own language, story, dance, love, work, and life as a Black woman. To her, one of the powers of eroticism, perhaps the most important of them all, is that which emerges from an experience fully shared with another person.

The episodes of individuals rubbing their penises against my knuckles, masturbating in front of me, or showing me photos of their girlfriends' pussies are directly related to our powerless bodies and to a lack of eroticism. When it comes to their own bodies, their power is considerably greater than mine, and they decide to wield it for their own benefit, forcing my body to participate in their sexual act without giving me the option to consent — or to reject an unshared sexual experience. If I had been offered this opportunity, I never would have allowed my body to participate in an unshared sexual experience, which means that all of these episodes constitute abuse.

As soon as I grasp this truth, I recover the rage and outrage of my teenage years and early twenties. But this time I manage them differently: first, because I don't believe in rage as a weapon of mass destruction, and second, because I have two teenage kids I must teach to navigate their sexuality in terms of power — not only for their own good, but also for the good of the people around them. My anger has changed: I still don't hide it, not even from my children, but now it also affirms me as a mother, because it's compatible with love and care and joy: they nourish and define each other. My rage is regenerative.

In my house, you'll never hear the phrases *act like a man* or *behave like a lady*, because that would suggest a specific model of behavior as a man or woman, each with its own power, assigned at birth and determined by genitalia. These fixed categories would inevitably lead to fallacies along the lines of *boys don't cry* and *women don't know anything about cars*: arguments that only bolster the Fatherly Trinity, in which capital-m Men and capital-w Women are monolithic entities with specific functions and immutable behavioral codes. Faced with this ridiculous dichotomy, we try to teach our kids to see life as an experience shared by *people*. That is, we educate them against abuse and in favor of consent in everything they do, especially when it comes to intimacy and sex.

The challenge of raising children unbound by the ties of the Fatherly Trinity and aware of their own power — never abusing it, always demanding consent for themselves and for others — is vast. It calls on us to respect our own nature, and theirs, so that, in turn, they will learn to respect themselves and the people around them, independently of their gender and/or sexuality. It also requires us to show our son — not just out daughter — that he can and must access his own emotions, feelings, and sensations as a source of power and knowledge: in order to understand and respect himself, and in order to understand and respect others in the shared experience of life.

BETWEEN THE SOURCE AND THE GROUND

As far as I remember, the first expulsion my body ever experienced was an electrical one. It happened as I was playing with some friends in the room adjacent to the garage at home: a lodge-type basement with brick-and-mortar fireplace, bar, benches. The only living object in that white, diaphanous space, designed for celebrations, was an electric wooden piano that was plugged into the wall with two stripped wires, haphazardly jerry-rigged, whenever anyone wanted to play it. The first thing you had to do was make sure — this was the most important part — that the piano was switched off before you inserted each wire's long copper filaments into the corresponding hole. To unplug the thing, you had to repeat the same operation backwards: after making sure the piano was off, you'd tug on the two slender leads dangling from the socket and let them drop onto the cement floor until next time. When there were no adults around, the eldest sister was responsible for plugging and unplugging the piano. That meant me.

It was the seventies, when kids rode in cars without seat belts, got furtively drunk on the remnants of their parents' gin and cokes, and breathed in the dense cigarette smoke wreathing grown-ups as they chatted around the table and on long road trips to far-flung little towns where the grandparents lived. This rash upbringing left me with a split lip, my first mini-bender at age three, and an asthma that made its first appearance in adulthood — all entirely representative of the decade. I'd like to add a brief aside about the incident I'm about to recount: it took place in a household with a father who often had big ideas and rarely bothered with everyday details, and a mother of three children between the ages of three and eight who struggled not to succumb and disappear into the tangled mass of domesticity that, at this stage of marriage, in its totality and in absolute terms, was her responsibility alone. As a result, I imagine, in that house where our story is about to transpire, a plugless outlet coexisted with imminent electrocution.

It must have been Sunday because I was wearing my heavy pleated skirt, white tights, and blue shoes with the buckle on the side. Another reason why I suspect it was Sunday is because I was playing with an atypical group of friends, which meant we'd gone to some communion or wedding and then moved the party to our place, as usual. All the kids were horsing around in the basement when Jorge, two or three years my senior, took a seat at the piano and switched it on. When it didn't work, he turned questioningly to me. I explained that it had to be hooked up to the wall and made sure that the rest of the group, all younger than we were, would move away from the socket.

Then I looked at Jorge very solemnly and asked him to double-check that the switch was off and not to play it again until I told him so. But Jorge was overcome by curiosity, or by the confidence of being older or a better wire-expert than I, and just as I was preparing to thread the second wire into the socket, he flicked the switch.

Decades later, with the wisdom granted by Google, I set out to study the physiology of electrical expulsion in medical and engineering sources like the Merck Manual and the website *desenchufados.net* (unplugged dot net, if you will). I learn that I experienced a low voltage electric discharge of 220 volts, and that such discharges are only considered high voltage starting at 500. That electrical currents can be direct, like with batteries, or alternating, like in household electric circuits. That the direct ones travel in a single course and the alternating ones change direction fifty to sixty times per second. That's how I determine that the current expelled by my body was an alternating one. According to the Merck Manuel, this is the most dangerous kind, because instead of causing, as a direct current would do, a sin-gle muscular contraction, often intense enough to dislodge the person from the source, it triggers a continuous muscular contraction that can prevent the person from releasing their grip. I learn that, since the alternating current is constantly changing direction, instead of using commonplace terms like *entry* and *exit*, we should say *source* and *ground*. I also discover that, depending on the duration of exposure, the current passes through different thresholds, each with the body's corresponding reaction phases — and that these reactions can range from burns, to muscular contractions powerful enough to throw a person onto the ground, to cardio-respiratory arrest. It turns out that the body is a phenomenal electrical conductor and, since electricity tends to travel wherever it's met with least resistance, it particularly enjoys traveling through nerves, blood vessels, and vital organs. I'm amazed to learn that electricity is extremely lazy, lacking mischief and even initiative. I don't even want to imagine what could have happened that day if it had decided to prowl more deliberately through the recesses of my eight-year-old frame.

All I remember about the moment when Jorge flipped the switch was a tremendous spark in my hand. The crackle was followed by the vacuum of unconsciousness. I don't know how long it lasted, that void, because I didn't talk about it later with the other kids who were there, my sole witnesses — but electricity and I must have traveled together through several thresholds in very few seconds, or fractions of seconds. I remember opening my eyes and finding myself lying flat on the floor. I remember a burning sensation in my hand, the charred fingers that had clutched the wire. My fingerprints were gone. I remember lifting my head and seeing that I was missing a shoe. I remember someone going to get it, returning it to me. Between the *source*, the *ground*, and the laziness of the electric current is a poorly tied shoe that saved my life. I remember looking at Jorge, wanting to say *that's what happens when you don't make sure the switch is off*, but I also remember saying nothing and running upstairs to throw my arms around my mother, leaving all the other kids behind: motionless, speechless, terrified, astonished.

My incursion into the physiology of electrical expulsion, besides revealing that the discharge I underwent that day was far more dangerous than what my parents initially thought, leaves me with more questions than answers. If what I always believed to be an electrical expulsion was nothing but an exercise in conduction, then is every bodily expulsion a conduction? And if so, where to?

I keep reading, and I think of other expulsions my body has exercised over the years. I think of the blood expelled as part of a reproductive cycle I learned to coexist with for many years before I really knew I wanted to have children. My first period, at age twelve, triggered a destabilization of my vagosympathetic system it took me thirty years to make sense of, and which I now live with on precarious terms, depending quite literally on the day: on the weather, on how many hours of sleep I got, on how active or stressed I am, on the current levels of domestic, logistical, and emotional complexity. Of the 420 egg-producing cycles I experienced during my fertile years, only two resulted in fertilization: three embryos. Two cohabited briefly in my uterus, although they didn't culminate in a twin pregnancy, just one. The others, by not completing their reproductive function, became heavy and painful periods. Now I have an intrauterine contraceptive device implanted in my body to halt the blood in which my life once slipped away, and to maintain, however delicately, my vagosympathetic system's fragile balance. Yes, this lesbian has an IUD! Oh, if only we women could have had a switch in our navels, like the piano in the basement, to turn on and off the hormonal circuit of fertility! The pain, which rarely leads to anything, we would have been spared!

When I consider the stubborn cycle of fertility that so seldom results in the formation of an embryo, I also think of my three embryos that, in turn, experienced their own particular conduction: one, an absorption into the uterus; the other two on being expelled, once their gestation cycles were completed, in the form of babies with two years and nine months between them. The first, via a surgical procedure when the umbilical cord was wrapped around the neck; the second organically. Two births, two brutal expulsions of two little bodies that represented, for me, the antechamber of a separation, a lesson in letting go that would end right there, where all the body's conductions are finished: in death and decomposition.

Viewed this way, the conduction of the reproductive apparatus seems to involve four possible variables: wanting to procreate, being able to procreate, not wanting to procreate, and not being able to procreate. All possible conductions, as well as the reconductions of the reproductive system, depend on their combinations. Our desire to be mothers (mine and my partner's), my right to make decisions on behalf of own body, the counsel of organizations such as the National Center for Lesbian Rights and the Human Rights Campaign, the support of our loved ones, and the ingenuity and courage to create and expand places where we could exist: all of this was essential in establishing options and reconducting them toward the procreation and formation of our family, toward dignifying my sexodissident body as a uterine home.

I return to this great cycle of reproduction in its postpartum phase and consider lactation as the expulsion of the mother's milk — another process that, for me, was reconducted with the help of a breast pump, due to the lack of physiological synchrony between my first baby and my body, and which I was forced to curtail the second when he was hospitalized at three weeks.

I think of the period's ruthless return, in the 418 cycles of fertilization reconducted toward bleeding because they didn't result in the expulsion of another life. I think again about the fragility of my vagosympathetic system, which didn't know how to manage the onslaughts of my abundant periods every twenty-eight, twenty-nine, thirty days.

Expel:
1. *To force or drive out.*
2. *To discharge from or as if from a receptacle.*
3. *To deprive of membership or rights in an organization.*

Contain:
1. *To have within; hold.*
2. *To have as a component or constituent part; include.*
3. *To check the expansion or influence of (a hostile power or ideology).*

If expulsion is the opposite of containment, expulsion may also be understood as a body's refusal to contain someone or something for any longer. And so, speaking from my own experience, symptoms like inflammation, vomiting, trembling, or crying become mechanisms of expulsion employed by the body to reconduct and thus express its nonconformity with something. That is, the symptom becomes a show of physiological nonconformity, like the yelling or tantrum of a body pushed to the outer limit of its tolerance; the symptom as the beginning or the end of a physiological coexistence; the symptom like an exhausted body filing for divorce, trying to adapt to its circumstances in the face of an impossible, irreconcilable relationship.

I must have suspected that my body wasn't tolerating surgical procedures after my first knee operation to repair my anterior cruciate ligament. My sister had experienced the same injury some years prior: her recovery was swift, and ten days later she was out and about again, doing rehabilitation exercises on the *mesa camilla* dining table and plucking grapes from the vines during the harvest, crutch in tow. When my turn came, I figured it would go as swimmingly for me as it had for her. But fate threw back its head and laughed at my assumptions. Ten days after surgery, I was still doing my PT exercises in bed and felt a terrible pain in my knee whenever I got up for the bathroom. At the time, I attributed the drastic post-op differences to the superpowers of my sister (who does possess them). But no: what I mistook for another of her superpowers was just my own body's inability to recover from trauma within the timeframes established by Western medicine.

I started to sense something unusual about my post-op experience after my first C-section, which I took far longer to recover from than other women I knew. My suspicions intensified with my second knee surgery, this time on the meniscus. After a month of physical therapy, the knee, swollen and hot, was still painful and operating clumsily. Butting heads until I got an appointment with the surgeon, he confirmed what I'd begun to appreciate, which is that I was experiencing an abnormal amount of swelling and should halt all activity, including physical therapy, until the inflammation eased altogether. Now that I understand my body's nonconformity with incursion by scalpel, the two of us get along much better, and we've learned to enjoy the long game of waiting and post-op reconduction. What's more, my body knows it can count on me because I'll try to spare it the unpleasantness of surgical procedures whenever I can. Care, now more than ever, is mutual.

I'm still stunned by the phenomenon of vomiting as a symptom of my body's impossible and irreconcilable coexistence with something. I blush to remember all the drunken nights that ended with my young self puking into the toilet before getting into bed so I could sleep horizontally before the spinning started. It causes me real sorrow, because by then I was already familiar with the symptom of vomiting as a bodily intolerance, and I had no problem with continuing to get absolutely plastered and then throwing up whenever I had to. My relationship with symptomatic vomiting had started long before, with my first migraines, when puking was sometimes all that could mitigate the lights, the curves of warped reality, the stabbing pain behind the eyes, the nausea. By age fifteen, I'd developed an incredible knack for prodding my fingers all the way into my tonsils and forcing myself to gag and expel the contents of my stomach — just to soothe the migraine, calm down, and get some sleep. If I knew that migraine-induced nausea was indicative of my body's intolerance to something, then how could I have failed to recognize my drunken vomiting as my body's scream, its tantrum, pushed to the limits of its tolerance for wine and Coca-Cola?

The technical term for what prompted me to vomit to keep the spinning at bay — that is, "alcohol poisoning" — was in the air at the time: it was constantly trotted out by the Guardia Civil at parties and concerts, in newspaper articles and radio broadcasts, in the anecdotes of refined conversationalists. What shocks me still is that it took me so many years to see my body as the victim of that intoxication: the very same body that sustained and contained my essence, that the years had made me more and more dependent on. If I am my body, if the body is the space of the self, then how could I have tortured it like that?

The other two symptoms that leap to mind as examples of bodily intolerance are crying and my essential tremor. I've experienced crying since my very first sob-fest as a newborn. I've only had essential tremor for a decade, though, and since our first encounter, as with crying, we've been inseparable.

The mechanism seems to be the same for both symptoms, since both expulsions — tears in the case of crying; expansive waves as rhythmic, involuntary motions in the case of essential tremor — are activated when my body is overcome with emotion, pain, exhaustion, or cold (in the case of the tremor). Essential tremor manifests itself throughout my entire body, except for my head and feet, and it acts as a kind of high-precision seismic alert system that documents my body's nonconformity with all of the above. I didn't understand the true price the body pays for powerful emotions until I started coexisting with essential tremor; until I started to feel its expansive waves through every millimeter of my flesh.

Sometimes the cries of a body pushed to the limit overlap with mine, as in experiences of orgasm, surprise, or rage. That's when I catch us opening ourselves to the world together in our primordial roar, which cuts across every convention and expectation and simply exists. In those moments, more than in any other, my body and I become one in the presence of my lover, Iniesta's spectacular goal in the World Cup final, or the asshole who tries to steal our car.

Electrocution, periods, childbirth, lactation, inflammation, vomiting, essential tremor, crying, moaning, shrieking: all are expulsions that answer to the body's — my body's — incessant attempts to conduct or reconduct something toward some other place or state in its journey through life: to prolong it, to tolerate it, and, with any luck, to experience it joyfully and comfortably. In the end, it very well may be that between the *source* and the *ground* we're nothing but bodies in transition; nothing but the particular conductions and reconductions of bodies activated according to the chromosomic survival manual that all bodies cling to tooth and nail: all of us, newborns, diabetics, obese people, pregnant people, skinny people, people in love, deaf people, drunk people, neurodiverse people, manic people, immunosuppressed people, people full of rage. . . .

When I revisit the scene of that miraculous 220-volt expulsion in the family basement — the first time my body introduced itself to me as finite matter, the wrapper around my essence — and I review the story with the perspective granted by fifty years of transit, I see myself in the faces of those kids who, if only for a few seconds, witnessed the fragile balance between life and its coup de grace. And I find myself as they were: motionless, speechless, terrified, astonished.

THE ROTTEN DEPARTMENT

---

1. It's not the first time that the professor has opted to teach in Latin.

2. Although the author (then a twenty-one-year-old student) can't prove it, she could swear that the professor's intent by delivering an incomprehensible speech in the Roman language was twofold: first, to demonstrate the limitations of his students' intellect; second, to mentally masturbate in public (the author recalls a look of pleasure on his face).

3. The student has been able to ignore the professor's twisted shenanigans until this date.

4. The incident in question as recalled by the author (henceforth referred to as "the incident") lasted only a few minutes, but it marks a before and after in her patriarchal imaginary. LINGUISTIC CLARIFICATION: the term patriarchal won't be incorporated into the author's vocabulary for over two decades, which means that, on the day of the incident, the student lacks the language necessary to discuss and explain the true significance of what transpired.

5. Intuition / Merriam Webster: *The ability to understand something immediately, without the need for conscious reasoning.*

6. Intuition / the student's own definition: *There are lines that shouldn't be crossed under any circumstances.*

7. Most of the students enrolled in the class where the incident occurred are young people who identify as women. This statistical data point is relevant in any evaluation of the incident and its consequences.

8. Textual citation from the student's journal on Friday, April 5, 1991 (approximately one year before the incident): "This college business gets darker and darker… I'm tired of this shit."

9. The student begins the 1991-1992 academic year, her fourth, after an attempt to drop out. Her mother has prevented this from happening with the now-epic line "The only thing your father and I can offer you is an education. We have nothing else to give." Had this conversation taken place in the present time, the author would have told her mother that "An authentic education, the real kind, is what you're already giving me at home, and the academic kind can't touch that with a ten-foot pole." But that day she says nothing and retreats to her bedroom to cry.

10. The student's long silence (which precedes the moment when she feels like yelling and shaking her fellow students) results from trying to determine whether what she has just heard the professor say aloud is, in fact, what the professor has said, or just a figment of her imagination. The silence is long because the professor has spoken entirely in Latin until a few seconds prior. The change in register from Latin to Spanish causes confusion and hinders comprehension of the message.

11. During the first couple of years, the smell goes unnoticed, but by the third, the student starts to detect a certain rotten stench when she walks through the door of the School of Journalism each morning. The stench is accompanied by the peculiar sensation of inhabiting a body that has no presence within the walls of the institution.

---

12. The fourth year is the year of the revelation, otherwise defined as the year when the student determines the source of the stench: both among the professors and the student body of the institution, the student discerns a) the Spain whose Franco- and post-Franco-era privileges have adapted to and even benefited from a decade of socialist government. This Spain feels and behaves as if it were formidably superior; (b) the Spain that started from the ground up two decades prior; that is, the Spain of the descendants of those who lost the war; (c) the Spain that views everything in terms of plunder; and (d) the Spain devoted, body and soul, to the democratic experiment. The professor may personify the subcategory of misogyny under one or several of the four abovementioned Spains. The author can't prove it, because she has no further contact with the professor after the incident.

LINGUISTIC CLARIFICATION: the terms *privilege* and *privileged* won't be incorporated into the student's vocabulary for over two decades, which means that in her fourth year of college she lacks the language to discuss and explain the true significance of the rot.

SEMANTIC CLARIFICATION: although she doesn't know how to name it, the student has a well-formed mental image of privilege as a concept in her country and of its surrounding artifice. Her understanding of privilege will evolve over time.

13. During the same spring as the incident, war has broken out in Yugoslavia, and both the professor and the student body are familiar with the testimonies of ethnic cleansing and the mass rapes of Bosnian Muslim women.

14. In *Frances* (1982), a film based on the life of actress Frances Farmer, the protagonist, of untamable body and mind, is ultimately subjected to a lobotomy following various psychiatric institutionalizations. In *Thelma and Louise* (1991), the protagonists, of undisciplined bodies and minds, are subject to a chase and end up throwing themselves off a cliff. Even though these are two of the student's favorite movies, she has never watched them again. The author believes that the student's refusal to re-watch the films is associated with the use of misogynist and institutional violence toward the subjection of the untamable and undisciplined woman's body.

15. Direct quote from the student's journal dated Tuesday, December 17, 1991 (several months before the incident): "I'm exhausted and ready. I think I can handle anything, or almost anything."

16. The student is familiar with the work of the Madres de la Plaza de Mayo in Argentina, who march in white every Thursday to uphold the memory of their loved ones forcibly disappeared during the dictatorship. She doesn't know, however, that during that same spring, in Belgrade, Yugoslavian women of all ethnicities, also known as Women in Black, march silently every Wednesday to protest war, militarization, nationalism, ethnic cleansing, sexism, and rape.

17. The incident comprises (a) three gestures: the professor speaking in Latin and fixing his eyes on the girls seated in the front rows, the professor smiling, and the professor addressing the boys, and (b) sixteen words: "look at them, sitting there, not a word, not moving a muscle, like raped Bosnian Muslims."

18. As the professor continues with his lecture, now in Spanish, the student debates between telling him off or shaking her female classmates to jostle them out of their self-absorption (the student has attempted both strategies in different contexts, albeit with poor results). The student listens, the student hesitates, the student argues with herself, the student gathers her things and walks out of the class, never to return.

19. There's a philosophical question that wonders *If a tree falls in a forest and no one hears it, does it make a sound?* Unwittingly, and by leaving the class, the student is saying (a) "Here there was a shameless asshole who opened his mouth to suppress a group of women and relish the suppression of others"; and (b) "I heard it."

20. The student emigrates to the United States with one incomplete on her transcript on April 9, 1996.

21. The student receives her university diploma on March 20, 2012, through a resolution issued by the college's credit panel, the Junta de Compensación de la Facultad.

22. During the war – according to the verdict issued by the International Criminal Tribunal for the former Yugoslavia, created one year after the incident and dissolved in 2017 – Serbian forces practice mass rapes on the Muslim women of Bosnia. The Court estimates that the victims may number between 20,000 and 40,000 women.

YOU KEEP LEAVING

And in the sixth year of living in the United States, my body said *We are going to be okay*. Just like that, in English, and I had to believe it, because by then I'd left almost everything behind so I could stay here with a woman. Well, everything except for the language, which kept infusing me, like an IV drip, with all of my Spains: the one I remembered, the present one (strange, remote), and the one I'd hoped for and dreamed of. I clung to the language as best I could: I became a translator. And the language, grateful, hung in there stoically as it lost its shine, until I finally sat down to write with a discipline honed through years of thirst, years of pushing it aside and putting life before writing as practice. Since my body wouldn't let me do very many things at once, and faced with the ever-present possibility of dying young, I preferred to die without having written over dying without having raised and accompanied children. So here I am: alive, the mother of two teenagers, working on my second manuscript, with the needle firmly inserted into my central IV line, the one that flows into the heart that still beats in Spanish when it can. But yes, clairvoyant as it's been so many other times, the body spoke to me in English, expanding the panorama of my life as if it had suddenly yanked off the blindfold of migratory experience and let the light to flood in: *I was* — por fin — *going to be okay*.

The shift in the language of the conversations between my body and me (also known as an inner monologue) is pretty common, although it usually depends on the country I happen to be in when the dialogue takes place. In general, then, it transpires in English when I'm in the US and in Spanish when I'm in Spain. When I return home (meaning always, because wherever I'm going, I'm always returning), there's an equidistant linguistic point that overlaps with the very moment when I board the plane, mostly occupied by native speakers of the destination (if it's Dallas, Philadelphia, or San Francisco, the flight's full of English-speakers; if it's Madrid, Spanish-speakers). As soon as I set foot in the cabin and hear the passengers' nervous chitchat, my brain changes register and continues in the other language, como si nada: the switch is automatic and unconscious, like a muscular reflex of the bilingual brain. Something similar happens in my dreams: in the US, I dream in English; in Spain, Spanish. Which makes me wonder, if I spend most of my days in English: why do I keep telling stories in Spanish after twenty-five years in this country? In the words of Maya Piña, a Mexican writer and editor who lives in the US: "In California, practically alone, writing in Spanish — you keep leaving in your own language, María! Why?"

At first, writing in Spanish kept me from giving up my only means of seeing and capturing the world. Over time, though, it became a kind of return, summoned by the blank page. That's how I came to write my first stories in the United States. Stories without so much of a hint of English, not a trace of my life in California; stories in which I'm always going back to Spain because I refuse to truly leave — as if my experience with writing went on uninterrupted by the fracture of emigration. I wonder if emigration, like grief, has stages of its own. And I wonder whether my early texts might be part of the first one, the denial stage, overlapping in turn with what Fernando Olszanski, an Argentine writer and editor living in the US, calls *the literature of uprootedness* — writing marked by an ongoing emotional connection with one's homeland. I imagine that this denial stage, or withdrawal, depending on how you look at it, would have lasted longer for me if not for the birth of our daughter, which occurred — and this is no accident — seven years after my arrival. That is, the year after I realized I was, *por fin*, going to be okay.

It must be true, what people say: that having children is like putting down roots. In fact, mine won't start growing in the subsoil of this land until our daughter's birth. From that day forward, and very slowly, her country starts to become my own.

In the years to come, the years when our son is also born and I barely have time to write at all, my fiction feels disoriented: I can't figure out where to put my characters, or who they are, or where they come from, or where they're going. This stage overlaps with the most intense years of motherhood, and I want to be writing, but I don't know where to start or how to find the energy to do it. And so, very much accordingly, I don't, and I devote myself to mothering — rooted in my language, my culture, my country.

Our kids grow up in a household laced with various migrations, and therefore multilingual, multicultural, multithinking. For one thing, all four of us are the children of immigrants: my partner of Portuguese immigrants; me, a United Statesian immigrant; and my kids, obviously, of a Spanish emigrant. What's more, I myself may be the gravitational center of the migratory experience in our home: the great-granddaughter of an emigrant (Navarra-Arizona-California), granddaughter of an emigrant (Galicia-Havana-California), daughter of an emigrant (California-Madrid-Guadalajara), and emigrant herself (Guadalajara-California).

It wouldn't surprise me if the intergenerational migratory experience stopped with me; that our children, given the choice, opted to stay close by, because they've nursed, from their mothers and grandmothers, the consequences of uprootedness. Maybe what they'll remember, besides the richness it's granted their lives, will be the nostalgia, the Christmas melancholy, the heavy sighs of the women who left and kept coming back with words, music, scents, flavors in tow.

My writing is located inside that center of gravity where my identities converge: besides my identity as a migrant, my identities as a queer woman, a mother, and the occupant of a body in pain. If the body is the limit of all my experiences, then what part does physical experience play in my writing? What part does it play in my language? What is its role? Does it demarcate language or encourage it? Or is language what demarcates or encourages the body?

Dissent 1. *To have or express an opinion different from a prevailing or official position.*

If I consider my physical experience from the perspective of territorial and linguistic dissidence, sexual dissidence, and a physiologically dissident body and experience of motherhood, I have no choice but to point out the shores, the margins as the space that links them together. In other words, it's in the vertices of shared reality and isolation that this writer finds her place, and it's in those spaces that her identities and her writing are born.

Viewed in this way, my writing and my language are simply tools for attiring and communicating an experience that can't always fit into everyday speech. Maybe this hybrid manuscript itself has been born of that search; of my desire to capture, in words, my experience of inhabiting a body on the edges. Maybe this search has also prompted my need to write in Spanish "in California, practically all alone," as a way to keep leaving, and thus to keep coming back — but also as a way to re-experience the homeland of my mother, grandmothers, great-grandmothers, and great-great-grandmothers: the ones who lived in Spanish. Because, yes, my language is North American, too. And most of all, it's a way to keep remembering that some stories don't fit certain lives, which means you need to make them up yourself.

If, as Rosa Montero writes in *La loca de la casa*, her autobiographical book on writing and imagination, "the essence of madness is solitude," and crazy people are "exiled from shared reality," then I live and write from a place of madness. It's a manageable madness, but madness nonetheless. That said, it can be liberating to realize that you'll never wholly belong to a place or a space, because the edge, the shore, is also the territory of possibilities and hope. The territory of "Contamíname," as sung by Ana Belén; the amalgamation and enrichment of human experience.

"The margins aren't beautiful and they're contested elsewhere," wrote Almudena Grandes in her final column for the Spanish newspaper *El País*. How true that feels. They aren't, but they can become beautiful: beautiful and pleasurable and luminous. I like to think that that's the shore I live on, the one where I feel most comfortable, where pain sometimes bursts forth — but from where, little by little, shoulder to shoulder, we inhabitants of the edges can keep expanding our shared reality and its stories.

After all these years in the US, I may dream in English, but I keep harboring my hope in Spanish. A queer woman's hope, among many other things.

EIGHT LETTERS

I spent the winter of 2009 stumbling between a makeshift triage station in a tent and medical appointments with multiple specialists, nursing a cough that persisted from November until April. I was misdiagnosed with swine flu, whooping cough, seasonal allergies, and a lingering cold. No one knew, including myself, that what my body was dragging along was the trauma of rejection, and that the relentless cough was the only way it could find to sound the alarm.

I started coughing in late November, but so sporadically that we didn't pay it any mind at first. During those years, the periods from October to December and March to May were devoted to managing our son's severe asthma, and so my cough, accompanied by no other symptoms but fatigue, was relegated to the background. Weeks passed, until one morning I realized I couldn't even speak, inhale deeply, or lie down without coughing so hard I doubled over and shook.

The result was, for the first time in my life, that I had to shut up. No more reading out loud or telling my kids how the world worked. Calls to Spain got shorter until they stopped entirely. Throughout my hours as a classroom assistant and working at the cooperative preschool, visiting my daughter's school, taking my kids to medical appointments, and all the other activities that made up my experience of motherhood, I had a terrible pain in my ribcage and was either quiet or coughing. There was no middle ground. That was, as I'll always remember it, the winter when speaking ceased and coughing won.

It all started with a ballot proposition in California that, after acquiring the necessary 700,000 signatures, was put to referendum in the presidential elections of November 4, 2008. The initiative, known as Prop 8 — supported by the Catholic and Mormon churches, as well as other religious and conservative lobbies — endeavored to amend the definition of marriage in the California constitution, reducing it to a union between a man and a woman, and thus conclude, once and for all, the nearly decade-long legal and legislative battle to include same-sex couples in the official definition of marriage. The short version of Prop 8 is that it wanted to eliminate same-sex couples' recently won right to marriage, approved by the state Supreme Court just months prior.

This wasn't the first attack against our right to marriage since I'd lived with my partner. In 2000, Proposition 22 — anticipating the growing social acceptance of same-sex couples and responding to the newly created legal figure of the domestic partnership, which also included such couples — had succeeded, following approval by referendum, in getting California law to define marriage as something exclusive between a man and a woman. With this victory, they believed the dispute had been settled. But in March 2008, the Supreme Court of California declared Prop

22 unconstitutional and legalized marriage between same-sex couples. Hence the emergence of the abovementioned Prop 8 in November of the year my cough began.

Over the decade we'd been together, my partner and I seemed to be trapped in a vicious cycle: first, the popular votes would deny same-sex marriage, then the state courts would approve it. Congress had lacked the political courage to legislate it. Throughout those ten years, I didn't give a damn what my fellow residents of California, its legislature, or its supreme court might think, say, legislate, or sentence with respect to my relationship with her. What's more, marriage — a flimsy little eight-letter word that kindles so many passions — was an institution I'd sworn never to belong to.

As I once saw it, getting married would have meant giving in, succumbing to inertia, renouncing the labor of respecting and caring for one another. What's more, it had been obvious to me since childhood that marriage was a contract between two highly unequal parties, in which the woman, whichever way you looked, always stood to lose. In the late seventies, I still wasn't familiar with the term *power dynamics* — this language wasn't yet my own — but the concept was evident to me, and I witnessed it every day. I'm amazed to think that I wasn't yet ten years old when I came up with what remains my vision of marriage.

If I cared so little about matrimony and had no intention of getting married myself, then why was I hacking my lungs out because of a vote over same-sex marriage?

At first, my opposition to the constitutional amendment was purely rational: it was about defending the basic principle of equality. That is, supporting the equal rights, responsibilities, and opportunities for all people, including sexo- and/or gender-dissident people like me. It was about safeguarding the rights of people like me to get married, even if I wasn't personally interested in doing so.

Until the morning when our city turned up papered with signs in favor of Prop 8, including the hare-brained arguments that claimed our right to marry was an attack on other people's freedom of religion and expression, an offense against other parents, and, most of all, a danger from which children must be protected. None of these utterly unfounded arguments was new. The novelty was how they affected my affective circles and the life we shared. In other words, these people had decided that, in order to protect and defend their own children, they'd be attacking ours. And they were going to do that in our own home, on the streets we walked and drove each day. Our own neighbors, even: Mormons who had always smiled and treated us with respect. Until the crusade for that ridiculous eight-letter institution transformed them into strangers, armed them against the two neighborhood lesbians and their three- and five-year-old kids.

The only relief I recall from those days was that my children still couldn't read or fully understand what was happening around them. They knew, because we'd told them, that there was something called a bill that wanted to eliminate our right to marriage, and that their mothers were involved in an electoral campaign to make sure it wasn't approved. They also knew how to take a stack of lawn signs their mothers planned to distribute the next day and build an entertaining circle in the front yard, which they danced around, laughing and yelling *No to 8! No to 8!*

The first thing I'd done, inspired by a friend's pickup truck, was buy a white sign maker and write in huge letters *Prop 8 hurts my family* on the back windows of my car. I'd decided that, if this Spanish lesbian mother in the California suburbs had to drive fifteen or twenty miles a day, then the least she could do was turn Ford Focus station wagon into a campaign vehicle for the cause of equality.

We bought pins and stickers and handed them out to the few people we knew would have no problem flaunting them on their clothes, bags, and car fenders. We wrote postcards and emails explaining what the proposition really meant and sent them to all our friends and relatives. My friend (owner of the pickup, mother of a young son, wife to a woman; they'd married that same summer, following the Supreme Court invalidation of Prop 22) and I went out one night to uproot hundreds of pro-Prop 8 signs from public spaces, because we could no longer bear the stomachache we got whenever we left home. I hid the signs under our daughter's bed for months, afraid that the neighbors would find out if I threw them away. After all, many of those neighbors had helped pay for them.

We made our own signs out of cardboard boxes and drove out to the highway exit to stir the civil conscience of people heading home from work. I organized a protest at one of the city's busiest intersections. This was before social media, but twenty or thirty people I'd never met showed up and shook their signs for hours in the rain. I'll never forget the supportive honks from passing cars, especially those of the total stranger who drove up and down the road, windows rolled down, screaming his head off and honking so often that we too wound up shouting with joy whenever we saw him coming — cheering him on instead of the other way around.

One night in late October, mere days before the election, I went to bed with the conviction that the plot and spirit of my first novel would germinate from the essence of the last weeks. That's how *Patricia sigue aquí* was born — a story of love and survival against all odds — published in Spain a decade later by Editorial Egales. *Patricia sigue aquí* isn't the novel I intended to write, but the one I had to write — if I was going to narrate what was happening in the background of the winter when speaking ceased and coughing won. It's the novel I had to write to keep from going mute.

"the blood's flight to the place of all protest that's asthma"
(Silvia Goldman)

On an intellectual level, I'd understood perfectly well what had occurred during the campaign months; that's why I was able to novelize them. Physiologically, though, that would take a few more weeks to set in. The violence of its manifestation and the length of its aftershocks, as it devolved into chronic asthma, made me want to explore what my body was going through.

I knew the trauma affecting me physically had been collective, not just individual. A few days after election day, when we lost our right to marriage by a 4.48 percent margin of votes, I attended the post-mortem meeting held by Our Family Coalition, the organization devoted to supporting and defending dissident families like mine. We'd been members for years. Our daughter and I had marched with them two years earlier in the San Francisco Pride Parade, which was among the most thrilling moments of my mothering life.

The goal of the meeting was to review what had happened, take note of what had gone well, and learn from our mistakes before the next electoral onslaught, which was obviously on its way. But the gathering quickly became a painful session of grief for the victims of Prop 8 and their campaign: our families. That night, I realized that pain was communal, which later helped me grasp the reality that trauma, by extension, was also shared.

I studied collective traumatic experiences and their effects. As I read, I learned that there are two types of collective traumas: *social* trauma, which refers to a historical process or event that affects an entire population (like, for example, the trauma of the pandemic unleashed by the covid-19 virus); and *psychosocial* trauma, which originates in society itself and affects people or whole communities (like, for example, the trauma of racism, sexism, or lesbophobia). *Psychosocial* trauma, moreover, feeds on the relationship between the affected people or communities and society, and it's sustained by the institutional, group, and individual interactions they engage in. That is, the very existence of these people or communities in society reinforces and perpetuates trauma.

The traumatic *psychosocial* potential of an event depends on its characteristics (namely, how sudden, repetitive, protracted, and intentional the trauma is), on personal experience, and on each person or community's ability to react. I'd underestimated the traumatic potential of my sex-gender dissidence — and of that election — until the cough took its toll, becoming chronic asthma.

An event is psychosocially traumatic when the experience constitutes a threat to someone's physical and/or psychological integrity. When people call you a butch or a dyke in the schoolyard or local playground; when they constantly ask why you don't have a boyfriend — until you just make one up so they'll leave you in peace; when they say it's disgusting for two women to be together; when they insist on leaving you off all the forms you're forced to fill out to live in society; when you have to travel with copies of your children's birth certificates in your pocket; when people look you up and down and ask where the father is; when you realize that your son's classmate, who has come over to work on a homework assignment, won't set foot in your house ever again, because you saw the look on her mother's face when she learned that he has two moms.

An event is psychosocially traumatic when the experience leaves an indelible mark on the affected person or community: when you're a girl, but others think you look or act like a boy; when you're bisexual, lesbian, queer; when you come from a family with two mothers and no father.

An event is psychosocially traumatic when the experience has an unnarratable, unshareable, incomprehensible quality in other people's eyes: when you realize that your friends and loved ones (and don't even get me started on strangers), no matter how much they suffer on your behalf (and some suffer a great deal), will never understand what it's like to live like you. They'll never understand what it means to live together and start a family, dodging or overcoming thousands of obstacles just to live a normal, ordinary life. They'll never understand what it means to have a social worker show up on your doorstep and assess your home and your relationship so that the non-biological mother can adopt her own daughter. They'll never understand what it means to finally earn a right, only to have it snatched away again by your own neighbors, your coworkers, your kids' teachers. . . .

An event is psychosocially traumatic when one or more of the basic assumptions that constitute a person's sense of security are broken, especially the sense of invulnerability and control over their own life: when you discover that your acquaintances, the mothers and fathers of your children's friends — parents who speak to you politely at after school pick-ups, at birthday parties, at sports events — have funded the campaign against your right to marry, making donations of up to a thousand dollars; when your neighbors put out signs defending Prop 8 outside their own homes; when a neighbor one street down hangs, on her baby's stroller!, the largest sign you've ever seen against your right to marry and insists on parading it around every single day on her way to school.

So I'm not fooling myself: the election didn't cause *psychosocial* trauma. That kind of trauma started brewing long before, in a schoolyard and the town playground, and it continued all the way into the hospital where your children were born, and into their school, into the baseball or soccer team they played on, including all the times you and your partner had to duck out of sight to give each other one simple kiss on the mouth over the decade you've been together.

The straw that broke the camel's back, the nail in the coffin that triggered this trauma for me, was the collapse of our day-to-day life, of the small safe home we'd built with love and presence, patiently and rigorously anticipating every possible roadblock. What happened in the winter of the cough was that the veil of manners and decorum was drawn back, that the jaws of moral uprightness lunged at our jugular. They told us that the lives built by people like me stay standing upright by the grace of miracle alone: they're precarious, and at any moment, the storm winds of moral superiority, ignorance, and indifference, blown by the institutions and communities we live in, can sweep them away.

A SEISMOGRAM OF MY TREMORS

The first seismic event takes place on one of those early mornings when my drowsiness, my thoughts, my freshly brewed coffee and I are still soothing ourselves awake. I walk to the table with a steaming mug and notice that the liquid sloshes in my hand, as if jostled by something. Odd, but I assume it has nothing to do with me and put it out of my mind. A few days later, I see the same little current as I lift the mug to take the first sip of the day. That's when I realize that I'm the origin of the shaking after all. I steady the mug, gripping it with my left hand as well, and resting both my elbows on the tabletop; the liquid goes still and the coffee meets my lips at last. Once I've finished, I stand up, extend my right hand, and take a look. I could swear I see it trembling. The movement is nearly imperceptible, but it's there, no doubt about it. It's incredible to me that the coffee registered it before I did. I tell myself that there's no need to panic, I saw this sort of tremor in my mother's hands some years ago, on a summer afternoon in Spain, sitting together at the little table in her apartment to share a second cup of coffee. That summer, we thought her tremors must be a side effect of one of her medications. On the morning I register the first tremor of my own, I realize it's not a side effect at all, but a genetic flaw I've just inherited from her a bit prematurely: my mother experienced her first tremor at sixty; mine came at thirty-nine.

This initial, barely perceptible seismic event is preceded by another of far greater magnitude. But that one was never documented as such, because it occurred years before, during the complicated labor that eventually resulted in the birth of our oldest child. When I reach the hospital, I've been having contractions for nearly twenty-four hours and my water has just broken. The night drags on as the midwife monitors the baby's erratic pulse, suspecting it may be caused by complications with the umbilical cord. To avoid a C-section, she suggests an amnioinfusion (which isn't some kind of fancy tea, but the instillation of fluid into the amniotic cavity via catheter) to help the baby float, and thus, with any luck, get the umbilical cord to unwind wherever it's coiled. Thus begins the sequence of twists and turns I'm supposed to undergo in the hospital bed on my midwife's orders. As she hovers by the monitor, and during the gymnastic mayhem attended by the nurse and my partner, I wonder aloud how many centimeters I've dilated. I feel like a warrior willing to do whatever it takes for this baby, our jelly bean. They don't have a name yet: we didn't want to learn their biological sex, didn't want to burden it with colors or expectations or a personality. This baby will be whoever they need to be, and we'll be right here to love and accompany them along the way.

I return from my second and a half of mental meandering to the visceral experience of childbirth when I notice the midwife's eyes on me. I feel strong. I'm sure she'll say I've dilated six, maybe eight centimeters, and I'm sure the jelly bean will exit my gestational sac in a couple of hours, and I'm sure they'll come out crying and wailing for milk, and I'm sure I'll be able to see their face, and I know they'll tell us who they are.

"María, you're three centimeters dilated," the midwife says.

"What time is it?" I ask, and try not to crumble.

"Three a.m."

I could cry. Thirty hours of contractions for three fucking centimeters. Not even a tennis ball could make it out of there! I fight back tears: this warrior's reaching her limit.

"I think I need the epidural."

When, following the anesthesiologist's instructions and assisted by the midwife and my partner, I struggle upright and sit on the edge of the bed, I start to shake uncontrollably. They ask if I'm cold, and I say yes, but I don't think that's why I'm trembling. I don't know what's going on, I tell them; I've never experienced anything like it before.

"María, if I'm going to insert the epidural, I need the shaking to stop. Do you think you can do that?" the anesthesiologist asks.

"I'm not sure," I reply, shaking and shaking. "I'm trying as hard as I can."

My whole body shakes; it feels like I can't control myself at all. The midwife and my partner hold me down as firmly and lovingly as anyone could while the anesthesiologist maneuvers the miraculous injection that will lead me to the final stretch. The finish line, still remote, will be the operating room, where our jelly bean will make their way into the world via emergency C-section, and I'll be able to see their face the very moment of their birth, thanks to the epidural that required an entire team to inject.

Now I know that the theatrical and involuntary tremors during our daughter's birth are known in seismology as foreshocks. Although they weren't properly recorded at the time, I have no doubt that those tremors on March 1, 2003, were a premonition of the ones — more placid, more discrete — that would come later.

Eighteen years after this experience of childbirth, my body shakes. It shakes every day: my hands shake, my arms shake, and my legs shake; even my torso shakes. The only parts of my body that don't currently shake are my head and my feet. I think of the San Andreas Fault, just thirty kilometers from where I'm writing these words: the longitudinal fracture that cuts across California from north to south, traveling one thousand two hundred kilometers of seismic vulnerability.

I think of the Hayward Fault, the most active in North America, and the hundred twenty kilometers of seismic vulnerability where our house is perched. I think of my own fault. Where in my body is the fracture that unleashes such widespread seismic waves? How long is it? How deep?

Essential tremors are a neurodegenerative disorder, so now I know the fracture is located in my brain. My neurologist confirms this after over half an hour of questions and exercises I have to undertake in front of her as I try to read her face. I fear that the neurodegeneration could be more advanced than I think, that the tremors might be just the start of something insurmountable. I analyze her expressions as she analyzes my tremors. We're both looking for answers.

She explains that tremors are measured by their range and

frequency: the ones in my right hand have greater frequency and are thus more notable, but the ones in my left hand have a greater range. I wonder about a Richter scale for essential tremors, wonder how it would measure mine. These are the questions I ask no one but myself, because I don't actually want to know. For now, I settle for feeling and seeing the effect of the jolts: the glass that breaks as I wash the dishes, the necklace I can't clasp, the needle that someone else has to thread for me, the screwdriver that only fits into the head of the screw on the third try, the torso that shudders gelatinously inside and keeps me up at night… my handwriting that, like a seismogram, indelibly and degeneratively documents each of my vibrations on the page.

The primary cause of earthquakes is the interaction between the tectonic plates into which the earth's crust is split. But there's another lesser-known cause that interests me far more in its resemblance to my own tremors. As it happens, any process that produces large amounts of energy contained in rock is capable of causing an earthquake. And it's this process of releasing the energy contained in the form of seismic waves that has such a kinship with my own. The only difference between me and earthquakes is that, instead of releasing energy, I release adrenaline.

Adrenaline is a relatively simple molecule that, once loosed into the bloodstream, prepares the body to react to stressful situations. Considering its relative simplicity, adrenaline is marvelously prolific: it activates the circulatory system by raising blood pressure, improves the circulatory system's ability to dilate the bronchial tubes, and stimulates the production of dopamine, one of the happiness hormones. The half-life of adrenaline is two minutes, but the body can feel its effects for up to an hour after. Adrenaline is also my tremors' daily bread, the cause of all my earthquakes.

What I didn't know and have discovered since my tremors started is that the suprarenal glands secrete adrenaline for everything! You're tired? Not to worry: I'll send you a little fix of adrenaline in just a sec so you can keep on keeping on. Just had a fright? It's all good: here's another little shot so you can face the danger your brain feels besieged by. Stressed, worried, overwhelmed? Have another fix so you can defend yourself from what's obviously threatening it. Cold? Here's a double shot so you can reactivate that circulatory system of yours; we don't want you to get hypothermia. My brain doesn't care if I'm exhausted because I couldn't sleep one night, if I'm startled because the alarm went off when I was deep in slumber, if I'm nervous because I have to participate on a panel in front of an audience, or if I'm cold because I went out with my partner and forgot to wear a long-sleeved shirt.

Until this point, my body releases adrenaline like any other. The problem is when my neurological fault amplifies the effect of the adrenaline in the form of microquakes that shudder through me from head to foot without me being able to do much of anything about it. The intensity of my tremors depends on several factors, some of which are indeed under my control. That's where I prefer to center my time and energy. With the help of my new neurologist (the first one retired), the International Essential Tremor Foundation, Google, and my mother (whose experience is somewhat different; she only gets tremors in her hands), I design earthquake-resistant strategies to fight off the harshest symptoms, or at least their most intense repercussions. I get eight hours of sleep a night — with seven or less, I'd shake all day long. I drink from the heaviest cups and glasses we own, use the heaviest cutlery. I find some pens at Target that weigh quite a bit and help steady the zigzags when I write, and I keep them all over the house, in my writing shack, even at work. I buy a wristband packed with little lead balls and wear it to sign books. I regularly do resistance training and lift weights; better muscle tone, better physical control over my tremors.

Still, I've learned that the most important work I can do to cope with the magnitude of the quakes is managing my emotions. Which doesn't mean you stop feeling, but that you decide how you want your emotions to affect your bodily function.

In earthquake resistance work, it's essential not to make predictions, calculate probabilities, or anticipate events. The same thing is true with essential tremors as with earthquakes: we're absolutely certain that they're going to happen, and we know more or less where. What we don't know is when or how, and all we can do is be prepared.

CATHEDRALS

I spend Saint John's Eve, 2014, driving to Santiago de Compostela, where I'm going to meet my partner and stay for three days. I drive north on the N-VI highway and pinch myself, still confounded by my luck. No, it's not a romantic tryst or a pilgrimage — though it could be, considering all the planning and energy it's required to make it happen. I'm driving my sister's car, which is more like an early twentieth-century stagecoach, a 140-horsepower mega-car with three rows of seats acquired so that my mother could travel comfortably in the company of my sister, not to mention the gaggle of grandchildren. During the summers in Spain, my sister's stagecoach is a party on wheels. And this summer in particular, she's loaned it to me for a very special trip.

I drive with my nose pressed to the wheel, because this tremendous Meccano isn't made for humans of my height, and because I'm wearing my ubiquitous flip-flops, forcing me to hunker down even closer to the car. My mother can't stop smiling in the passenger seat. Every so often she turns and says something to my children, age eight and eleven, sitting in the middle seat. They smile and sometimes respond; their conversations, songs, and games shift back and forth between English and Spanish with striking ease. Here everyone expresses themselves as best they can, and the result is the bilingual mishmash I know so well, the soundtrack of our Spanish summers. Looming beyond their heads is everything we need for our big journey: bags of clothing, a couple toiletry kits, the pool bag, medications, my son's nebulizer; my mother's oxygen machines (the portable one and the one for the house), wheelchair and walker. Ready for anything!

That same day, my partner and her mother are also driving north, but setting out from Portugal. They've traveled from the US to Spain's neighboring nation a few days prior. They've lost half a day wheeling along to the *tun-tun* beat of the rented car that, algorithmically and on its own initiative, leads them from one regional highway to another to avoid paying the toll on the major freeways, transforming what was supposed to be a half-hour pilgrimage to Fátima into a three-hour Portuguese ordeal. For my mother-in-law, who emigrated to California from the Azores archipelago at age seventeen, this is her first visit to the Portugal of the Iberian Peninsula. For my partner, too. It's a trip they longed to take for decades, their own personal journey. The soundtrack of their summer is an English-Portuguese mishmash.

Our mothers met in the United States a few months after we did. The long periods my mother spent living in our house — for the births of our children, and during the California winters, which turned out to agree with her health far better than the Spanish ones — solidified their friendship. My partner and I are the daughters of emigrant women: her mother fled poverty to the US a few years before my own mother left the US for what was initially meant to be a one- or two-year stint in her father's country of origin. As young children, we both absorbed our mother's stories, sayings, and nursery rhymes in a foreign language. She grew up as the Portuguese couple's daughter, I as the daughter of the *americana.* My mother and my partner, both American, have much in common that has helped them bolster their bond. I, the Spaniard, have lots in common with my Portuguese mother-in-law: our Mediterranean culture and traditions have brought us closer.

By Saint John's Eve, 2014, my mother and mother-in-law haven't seen each other for several years, since my mother can no longer fly. The final destination of our drives is the single-story house — not a stair in sight — we've rented in a village on the outskirts of Santiago. That's where we'll spend the next few days all together. Galicia, here we come. *¡Aquí chegamos!*

After a first day of chatter, food, coffee, lingering at the table after meals, dips in the pool, walks out and about, and visits to the bar in town, we pile into the stagecoach and drive to the city. Our only ambition is to see the cathedral; with a crew as motley and scattered with impediments as ours, we couldn't ask or plan for much else. Deep down, I think the cathedral is the least of it: what we want most in the world is just to be together, and we are. I look at us in the rearview mirror and picture us connected by invisible threads, crisscrossed and interwoven into hundreds of ligaments and combinations, some fairly predictable and others that would have been unimaginable just a few years earlier.

I wonder what kinds of fibers form our disparate and colorful fabric. If I had to guess, if I had to answer right off the top of my head, I'd say they're love, devotion, and an enormous margin of error. We're erring and errant folk.

The streets adjacent to the Cathedral are blocked to traffic. I determine that the only way my mother can make it to the Plaza del Obradoiro is by car; any local police officer will understand that. With the disability ID card in hand, just in case, I maneuver the stagecoach, skirting the cylinders blocking the way, and inch toward the Cathedral at zero kilometers an hour, windows down, very politely asking all pedestrians to help us get through. Inside the car, the silence is absolute. As soon as we enter the plaza, there's a collective sigh of relief and the trilingual mishmash starts up again. "Your father and I slept here on our honeymoon," my mother tells me when I park in front of the Hostal de los Reyes Católicos. We glance at each other and smile. I leave her reminiscing about more mobile times and go get the wheelchair. As I open the trunk, I discover that one of the tires is flat — or worse, punctured, and the chair doesn't come with a pump. I sigh with relief once again when I see that some of the pilgrims are rolling in on a bicycle. I approach one, explain the situation, and he loans me his. I inflate the wheel and wait. The thin tire holds the air and my mother can finally get out the car. My partner goes to park and the rest of us stay put in the middle of the plaza, admiring the Cathedral. It's a remarkable sight, even in the eyes of this incorrigible atheist who's visited countless European cathedrals and sees nothing in them but the formidable architectural culmination of centuries of social, political, and economic abuse — the ecclesiastical enterprise should be an object of study in economics and political science programs. I tell myself all of this as I admire the magnificent building and consider the best way to get the whole group of us inside the cathedral. My mother solves the dilemma for me when she says she actually isn't all that interested in going in — she's seen plenty of cathedrals and would rather stay outside with the pilgrims. My partner soon shows up and we make a quick decision: my mother will stay put in the square, my partner will accompany her own mother into the cathedral, and I'll take a walk with the kids to burn off energy and show them the old city.

We wander around the square for a few minutes as I watch my mother out of the corner of my eye. I've left her by the porticos where the newly arrived pilgrims are gathering, and I want to make sure she doesn't need anything else before we head out. Just as I suspected, she's chatting up a storm and it hasn't even been two minutes. I relax and we start out on our stroll. I lead, followed by my daughter, who watches people as she goes, and my son takes up the rear, climbing up and down steps and the low walls that separate the plaza from the street below. I tell them why the streets are cobbled, how many centuries it takes to build a cathedral, and at whose cost, until we reach a little store with a coin-engraving machine. My children's eyes widen to recall how we recently engraved a penny in San Francisco with a machine much like it. I give them a few eurocents and they entertain themselves for a bit. We continue down the street until we reach a manhole cover I instantly recognize, stopping me cold.

It's possible to revisit the city where you had one of the cruelest, most violent experiences of life and not even remember — until you run straight into the blasted manhole cover! I turn to my kids, point to the ground, blabbering, and they stare at me. How can I explain that, twenty-four years ago, their mother took a terrible beating right here? On this very same sewage drain I can't even bear to step on!

That summer, I was visiting Santiago with my mother and a friend. We were crossing the city center on our way to the cathedral when we passed a young couple walking a bit erratically. The girl made an unexpected movement as she stepped over the manhole and my friend let out an innocent giggle. The girl bristled and confronted her. My friend tried to explain that she'd just reacted instinctively to something she found funny, but the girl insisted she was mocking her and raised a hand. I intervened and ventured, as calmly as I could, that the laughter wasn't malicious, my friend didn't have anything against this girl. But she didn't care about what I had to say: she was all fired up, itching for trouble. She grabbed me by the hair and yanked so hard I nearly fell to the ground. In a rush of instinct, my mother, one of the least violent people I know, clutched at the girl's hair, too. The triangular fit of hair-pulling lasted, I swear, at least two minutes.

The guy and my friend looked on, probably not sure what to do. I tried to convince my mother that if she let go of the girl's hair, she'd release me too, and there would be no need for things to escalate further. Not a chance, my mother replied: she wasn't letting go of her until the girl let go of me. In the end, who knows how, I persuaded her. But as soon as the girl was free, just as my mother had suspected, she lit into me. My mother started calling for help. The guy joined in and they both started assailing me with their fists.

From that moment on, I remember only certain details: my mother's attempts to join the tangle of punches and kicks to get them off me; her desperate screams for help; my friend dashing off in search of the police; finally landing on the ground after receiving a long barrage of blows; curling up to make myself as small as I could, shielding my head with my arms and my belly with my knees. I remember looking up when it seemed like the kicks had ceased and seeing, beyond my arm, dozens of silent feet surrounding us in a circle of tourists and passers-by. If this had happened today, I'm sure they would have recorded us on their phones and we'd have ended up all over social media. Seeing us on Twitter would have broken my heart.

My mother had begged all of those people to help and not a single one had made the slightest attempt at intervention. That's the moment I'll remember for the rest of my life: not the punches or the kicks I was dealt by two junkies in the vicious throes of withdrawal, but the indifference and passivity of at least a dozen adults who merely watched as I received a terrible assault. It would land me in the hospital, and it would keep my mother on high alert all night long: the doctors had told her to watch out for any sign of unconsciousness or stroke.

This isn't the story I tell my children when they find me stammering and gesturing wildly at the manhole cover. How to explain that their mother's foundation collapsed that day? How to tell them that the bedrock of what she believed hold us all up turned out to be a mere illusion — unfounded, some would say, and others simply laughable? It was a structure that had already started gathering serious cracks and fractures by the age twelve, losing soundness during her school years and college days. How to get it across to them that something in their mother broke that day, something it would take her decades to rebuild?

There's a pedagogical concept known as the *wonder approach to learning*. I first heard about it while talking with my Spanish sister-in-law. It has to do with accompanying children as they learn by paying attention to what their individual nature seems to need, respecting their innocence, their rhythms, their sense of mystery, their thirst for discovery. I was excited to learn that this was the kind of learning we were already facilitating at home, and I kept the name, which felt right on target. That said, I think the *disappointment approach to learning* is just as important, because life is full of disillusionment, deceit, and frustrations, and accompanying kids in their dawning awareness of the disappointment and cruelty all around them is just as crucial as attending to their realization of wonder. And so, beside the manhole cover that afternoon, I decide to spare them the unpleasant image of their mother curled helplessly into a ball on the ground and save that story for when they're a little older — for when, inevitably, they've started to discover the imperfections and vulnerability of the two women who brought them into the world, and the cruelty in their midst.

After what feels like an eternity of walking in circles around the old city, we make our way back to the Plaza del Obraidoro, where my mother is chatting animatedly with a group of pilgrims. She has always been a good listener. From her wheelchair, she asks questions and pays rapt attention to each and every tale told by the new arrivals. She introduces us when we come over. There's a girl from northern Europe with a backpack at her feet, a young blond guy with a guitar, another wheeling up on a bike. They've been telling her about their *caminos,* and my mother won't forget the details for years — that's the kind of listener she is. Other people's stories sustain her; they always have. We leave her with "her" pilgrims, as she's already calling them, and walk over to the benches by the Hostal de los Reyes Católicos. We're soon joined by my partner and her mother. My mother-in-law is moved and impressed by the mass, the bishop, and the three priests in attendance, as well as the enormous incense-laden artifact swinging from the cathedral vault. "The bishop, three priests, and even the *botafumeiro,*" I echo. "You won the Catholic lottery: the pilgrims' mass!" My mother-and-law smiles with satisfaction and delight.

I think of the faith that sustains her, the hope she's always placed in that god, something none of the rest of us can identify with: my children, at least for now, have expressed interest in knowing more, but haven't absorbed her beliefs. Beliefs that continue to nourish her, even though they once denied her own existence and that of her lesbian daughter. I think of what sustains my partner.

At this point in our relationship, I'm convinced that she's

nourished by seeing her loved ones, and the people around her, treated with care and respect. I have no doubt that, if she'd been here twenty-four years back, she would have run to help my mother and me, two perfect strangers; she would have rushed to our aid, shouting and shoving. Who knows? Maybe other onlookers would have followed suit and the story would have had a different ending. Although half a lifetime has shown me that most people opt for indifference and passivity in the end, for standing comfortably in their everyday circles of tourists and passers-by.

The support of my mother, sister, and two or three close friends wasn't enough for me to rebuild my foundation. The first people to contribute collectively to this reconstruction were my handball teammates in Alcarreño de Balonmano (my sister among them). My years with these women showed me that the ligaments and other ties that bind us together can be as strong and solid as our differences. These were foundational years in my adulthood. Later, living in the US, my partner would appear. Some years after that, I'd join forces with my fellow mothers in the cooperative preschool, forging the alliances I needed to develop quite an unconventional view of early childhood education in those days. The five years I spent in the co-op, plus co-parenting with my partner, were also essential to my identity as a mother.

Now I'm also sustained by my daughter, and by other women writers through the creative alliances and mutual support we're weaving together with various ligaments and assorted bonds:

some fairly predictable and others that would have been unimaginable just a few years back. Even though I've had the support of men both magnificent and erring — my father, my brother, my son, certain friends — my support system has revolved and still revolves around my alliances with other women. They are my cathedral.

MOTHERING INCOGNITO

The professional closet is cluttered with difficult childbirths and messy scarring, diapers and spit-up, sleepless nights, emergency room visits, walks and outings, hugs and kisses, games and empty hours, exhaustion, love, terror, joy, doubts, sorrow, and — most of all — silences.

By chance, I stumble across the newly published anthology *A muchas voces: Escrituras desde la maternidad* [*In Many Voices: Writings from Motherhood*] (El Traspatio, Mexico, 2020). In an interview conducted by Adriana Pacheco for the podcast *Hablemos Escritoras*, the editors explain that, by organizing a compendium of 38 mothering voices, they sought both to demystify motherhood and offer accompaniment. After all, the exercise of motherhood is laced with solitude, even loneliness. Society, they say, expects us to raise children practically on our own — and with sky-high expectations.

Solitude is surrounded and nourished by silences, both those imposed by the environments we live in and those we impose on ourselves. Solitude thus becomes the price paid by most of us who mother. This becomes even more evident in the US labor market, the cradle of neoliberalism. Because caring for our loved ones and raising our children (with all the physical and emotional labor they entail) don't compute when it comes to the balance sheets, and because this work falls heavily on our shoulders, the great US productive machine relies on the belittlement of motherhood. In a country where nearly all women work and 86 percent are mothers, belittling motherhood means erasing the vast majority of mothers who want and/or have to work — that is, forcing us to mother incognito and in silence.

As a nation, the US simply isn't designed for working mothers. Mandatory education doesn't start till age six, public education till five, and any other kind of early socialization and schooling depends on family networks and the private sector. In other words, if you want to work and have kids in this country, you have three options. The first is to keep working and pay astronomical sums for daycare and preschool, which often eats up most of your salary. The second is to stop working when your kids are born, then reenter the workforce part-time once they start school — the option chosen by most middle-class women, especially when they have working partners who bring home a full day's wages. The third option is to leave your kids in their grandmother's care during the workday (ah, grandmothers, those re-mothering women submerged in their own silences). There's also a fourth option, but this one is only accessible to the most privileged of mothers: to stop working altogether. However, for women who actually enjoy their work, having to stop is a dubious privilege at best.

According to my mother, by the time I was five years old, I was certain I wanted to have kids someday — but would never get married. How can a five-year-old girl be so sure about such things? Now I know that childhood is marked by a natural intelligence that only contracts over the years, sometimes shrinking into outright stupidity, under the weight of silence. In the end, my adult reality hasn't much diverged from that early declaration of independence. I wound up falling in love and living with a woman. Together, we banked on a life and a family beyond the tethers of the patriarchy. Or at least that's what we hoped for. Today, two women can't live outside the patriarchy; at most, they can try to live in parallel. We decided to come out of the closet as lesbians and raise children outside of that closet. Which is to say, we are and have always been a visibly queer family calling for space to raise our two kids with love, hard work, mutual respect, and as much freedom as possible.

With a naïveté instilled by growing up in Spain, a country with national and universal health and public education systems (including low-cost daycare, schooling that starts at age three, and a social fabric far less eroded than in the US), I assumed that my professional reintegration after giving birth to our children would take a matter of months. A colossal mistake! My first foray into motherhood couldn't have been more different than what I'd imagined. Of the four options a woman in the US must choose from to be a working mother, I experienced basically all of them over a seven-year period.

The nice thing about creating a family in parallel to the patriarchy is that nothing about the family unit is taken for granted, which grants you an incredible capacity for maneuvering and improvisation.

For seven years, we improvised beautifully: it went great.

Well, not everything was beautiful, and not everything went great; let the record show that I'm not interested in mythologizing anything. The truth is, though, we spent those years as we wanted to, accompanied by little people who brightened and enriched our world beyond what I have words to express. It was a time when we had to learn how to inhabit this uncomfortable place on the edge of so many things: collapse, tragedy, joy.

At the end of this long and winding road, when our youngest started school full-time, I got ready to rejoin the workforce. The first thing I did was update my CV, the letter of introduction that was supposed to fling open the doors of the working realm once more. All it actually did for me, though, was send me right back into the closet — the professional one this time. There was a gaping hole in my resume that corresponded to the years I'd devoted myself entirely to mothering. They were a hole in my career, an inexplicable void that prompted anyone who wanted to hire or work with me to wonder: why had this translator stopped working? Was it something about the quality of her work? A lack of interest? Could she be a poor team player? Was she fired, or did she stop working voluntarily?

After that first CV as a mother, I've drafted quite a few more: as a translator in Silicon Valley, a literary translator, a freelance translator for nonprofits, a writer and journalist, a professional ready to embark on teaching Spanish at a community college, a professional ready to lead operations at a small publishing house… and not a single one of these CVs makes any mention of my full-time mothering years. Maybe they can be glimpsed between the lines, because my years of absence from the workplace overlap with the references I do make to my volunteer positions on the board of a cooperative preschool, as a volunteer coordinator of a support group for Latin American immigrant families in a public school, as a volunteer translator and interpreter for my local school district, etc. But I pursued those activities during the later years of motherhood, when my kids needed me less at home. Which means that those early years, the most difficult and most important for me as a mother, don't show up at all.

When I came out of the closet, I swore I'd never get into another one ever again. Even so, my CVs make no mention of being a mother — even though, ironically, it's been the hardest job of my life, and the one that has best prepared me for everything that would follow in my career.

I think the time has come for us to stop mothering incognito. I think the time has come for us to spotlight and account for the physical and emotional labor of mothers in the terms it deserves. The pandemic blew up the professional closet from the inside, and the whole world witnessed — on Zoom — the chaos, the impossibility imposed on working women as they try to fulfill both their parental and their salaried responsibilities without structural support and/or the commitment of a partner (if applicable) to co-parent their children.

Because what isn't named doesn't exist, I propose that we pull motherhood out of the workplace closet and put it on our CVs. I propose that we abandon the silence of motherhood and name it, name it, and name it.

A MAP OF THE BODY UNDER SIEGE: PANDEMIC 1

In late March 2020, with the covid-19 virus on the doorstep of the US, I decided to document the experience from a body under siege. I mapped my own body-territory, inspired by the way Latin American women, especially in the rural and indigenous context, have used bodily cartography to identify the aggressions suffered by the territories they inhabit. I also drew on the foundational idea that the body is our first territory, and that we recognize territory in our bodies. The model for this cartographic exercise is found in the document Mapeando el cuerpo-territorio: Guía metodológica para mujeres que defienden sus territorios [*Mapping the body-territory: Methodological guide for women de-fending their territory*] (Colectivo Miradas Críticas del Territorio des-de el Feminismo, 2017).

In writing this essay, I wanted to sketch a map I could return to if I ever lost my way in the violence of covid-19. I've since used it twice.

April 1, 2020 – Fremont, CA

My body: As I approach my fiftieth birthday, I find myself ac-companied by an anatomy that hasn't grown or regenerated for twenty-five years: a graying head of hair; finer and sparser body hair; coarse skin; a faltering memory; eyes that need glasses after a life of perfect vision; a stockpile of pounds around the hips and organs that birthed two children; periods suppressed by an intrauterine device, because over-abundant bleeding caused serious imbalances in my blood pressure; a post-op left knee I can no longer rely on for handball or soccer or dancing; a tremulous body, because that's what I got in the genetic lottery; assorted scars (on my heart, on my skin, and an enormous gash across my forehead that reminds me to never run around the house, especially not in my underwear); and let's not even bother to itemize the headaches and occasional bouts of vertigo, all intimately connected to how I perceive the world. Maybe I sometimes see and feel too much, and headaches are my body's way of begging me to stop looking for a while. I should mention that, much to my surprise, my physical decline has come with an unprecedented mental clarity that has, in turn, yielded one of the most intense, most powerful, and most generative times of my life. As the saying goes, I am, creatively speaking, *on fire*.

My territory: Ever since I was a teenager, and especially over the past decade, I have adapted my life, activities, and environment to the reality of an anatomy in decline; one that is genetically somewhat peculiar. I spent years working from home because my youngest son's health required it when he was small, and then mine did, too. (He and I are both members of what's known these days as the "high-risk population"; we both have troubled lungs, and I have a few other issues besides.) Until three weeks ago, I lived my life in spaces perfectly calibrated to preserve the fragile state of my biology, which is strong but prone to ups and downs. On Tuesdays, Wednesdays, and Thursdays, I commuted to work in San Francisco; I devoted Mondays, Fridays, and the occasional weekend hour to my writing and its adjacent activities (writing at home, in the library, in some nearby café; readings, lectures, etc.). Weekends and evenings were reserved for my partner, our two children, and our loved ones, scattered across two continents. As an immigrant, I spent many such hours on WhatsApp or on the phone to Spain (I'd usually chat with my mother as I washed the dishes; with my siblings, as I walked or biked; with my friends, whenever possible, never enough). I walked to the creek that cuts across my city when I needed to be alone; to the gym when I needed to strengthen my body, put it to work. I went to the grocery store for everything needed to live in this home, to the kitchen to nourish my people. I filled all remaining hours with appointments, emails, phone calls, and sundry ins and outs, because otherwise our domestic life would have lacked order and coherence. In the summers, we visited Spain and took a couple camping trips in the woods along the California coast, which restored my sense of peace and equilibrium. My partner and I occasionally broke away to have coffee, or shop, or wash the car, or take a walk, or eat dinner out — any excuse was a good excuse to spend a bit of time together, to remind ourselves and each other that, even amid the craziness of the day-to-day, we were still the same couple we'd been for twenty-two years. Every *x* number of years we'd pull off an actual escape for two or three days.

My body-territory: I've always kept my friends and family clasped to my chest, tightly swaddled behind my breastbone. My job in San Francisco and my writing have always clung tooth and nail to my backbone, holding me up. The creek, the surrounding hills, and the redwood forests have always been an all-soothing embrace, like one of those gravity blankets that are currently in vogue. I've always worn the gym in my muscles; it's been my gasoline. Trips to the supermarket, my incursions into cooking, and the logistical, medical, and emotional care of my children have always been both my desire and my duty (a desire and a duty I share with my partner): a primitive, almost animal desire-and-duty, a desire-and-duty that were never questioned but simply enacted and endured, full stop. As such, I'm not quite sure where they've nested in my body — probably at the cellular level, the most ancient one of all. I've always carried my partner symbiotically inside and outside me at the same time: we're two very different women who found a way to "make it work" for ourselves and for our queer family. We've always faced everything together; together, too, we've taught our children to live with dignity in the maelstrom of the lesbophobia, ignorance, and prejudices of acquaintances, our kids' classmates and their parents, coworkers, politicians, the bureaucratic system, strangers, and even our next-door neighbors (we live in a Mormon neighborhood). Together, we've showed them that honesty and respect — for others and for themselves — are essential.

Pain, fear, and shame were inevitable. Pain slowed and darkened the world for me; it seeped into my body, and I've doubled over with it. In the presence of fear, my body-territory has felt it in my stomach, clenched in its cold iron fist, stifling every second of the day. I've been ashamed of my faults and the faults of others, because I always wanted us to be better than we were. I must say here, though, that I've never felt ashamed of my partner or our children. Only proud.

Every so often, my sense of equilibrium in the enterprise of living has collapsed, because my blood pressure has been thrown into turmoil and my body has switched off. On those days, I've had no choice but to retreat to the couch, elevating my feet, and submit to the passing hours with my head stuck in a book or a movie, or asleep. On those days, writing has never saved me, because there was no backbone to hold me up.

My body in coronavirus territory: My body-territory feels the state of alert at the most primitive level — the cellular level — on March 3, 2020, when I decide to not attend a writing conference in San Antonio that I've spent almost a year preparing for. This virus troubles us in a serious way. My partner and I spend the next week with our stomachs throttled by the fist of fear, plunged into a tsunami of emotions and extraordinary measures that we should almost certainly be taking, but which we still can't bring ourselves to carry out. Our amygdalae, incandescent with alarm, shrill at us to do something: if respiratory viruses, especially the flu-like ones, have always activated protocols in our family, and if covid-19 is a flu on steroids, then shouldn't we be pulling our kids out of high school right this minute? Shouldn't we all be staying home?

The history of our son's asthma began in an ICU in December 2005, when he was just five weeks old, and although his symptoms have grown milder ever since, they meant, for entire years of his life, weeks of confinement, inhalers and nebulizers, corticoids, alternative treatments, 2 a.m. phone assessments by ER doctors, whole nights holding him in an armchair to keep him upright, our own efforts to educate ourselves and prepare, yoga, writing, psychologists… He's always handled it well (the perseverance and optimism of kids with chronic illnesses is truly extraordinary); we're the ones who have had to learn to live with it. For some years now, I've had asthma, too.

By March 12, we've decided that our kids aren't going back to school and that we'll all voluntarily confine ourselves to the house. (I propose to my boss that I telecommute; my partner will have to keep going in to work at her company.) A day and a half later, the local schools are closed and we're all urged to stay home. Three days after that comes the shelter-in-place order for the entire state of California. Gabriela Wiener writes in the Spanish newspaper *eldiario.es* that "love is disinfection now." We've been practicing love by disinfection for fourteen years — which is precisely why the great migration toward the cleaning and pharmacy sections of the supermarket finds me ensconced at home, well-supplied with hand sanitizer, disinfectant wipes and sprays, and ample medication, in case we should both suffer a long-term asthma attack. Luckily, it also finds us with ample reserves of toilet paper, plus our emergency kit for earthquakes, which I'll have to restock with N95 masks and latex gloves as soon as I can. In this household, we've always washed our hands with particular diligence from September to April (flu season).

Now we're even more thorough. My partner and I enter into a state of total symbiosis. We're in survival mode, in act-as-calm-as-possible-without-concealing-the-gravity-of-what's-at-stake mode, another exercise we've been practicing for years. There's no doubt about it: we're prepared.

But after nineteen days of confinement, and after seeing the levels of covid contagion in Spain and New York, I realize that I'm actually not as prepared as I thought. My chest cavity, where I've always carried my family and friends, has buckled in distress. The backbone that has almost always held me up is sagging, yet not broken: I'm still working from home (although I know that our small, historic publishing house won't be able to sustain my role as director of operations much longer), and I've been writing, hence this pandemic account you're reading now. My muscles demand that I ride my bike, head for the gym. I start to worry about running out of gas. For now, and thanks both to the low population density of the area where I live and to the governor's directive, I can still take my walks by the creek. I do this every so often, very early in the morning, wearing a mask. The embrace of the sequoia forests, soothing as a gravity blanket, will have to wait. At home, we still hug, but we've stopped kissing each other on the face (I kiss my children on their foreheads or the top of their heads). My partner and I have stopped cuddling in bed. She's our contact with the outside world, which makes her our kryptonite. I'm in touch with the heaviness of my sorrow. Even so, I know that true pain and true fear haven't yet reached my body-territory, and that it's surely only a matter of time before they hit.

My struggle, my rebellion, my mobilization: Despite the extreme forms of planning I've alluded to, my struggle is a visceral one, because it's waged against fear and for survival. Ever since our daughter was born, I've always carried my courage nestled firmly against my ovaries. I must admit that I'm not quite sure where I carried it before then; maybe in some other organ, better hidden, less latent. I've lost heart a few times in these nineteen days. When my mood plummets, it's my rebelliousness that has helped me find my way out: the defiance that once made my kindergarten teacher cover my mouth with tape or prompted a nun to stuff the chalkboard eraser between my teeth when I was eleven years old. The same defiance that prompted me to walk out of a college history lecture, never to return, when the professor mocked the Muslim women being raped in the Balkan Wars. The same defiance that spurred me onto the streets to defend my right to marry. The same defiance that had me pull our kids out of high school without a second thought when my child's health and my own were at stake. I think my rebelliousness is my compass: I know that if I haven't rebelled for a while, it's because I haven't been paying attention. The world is full of injustices and if I don't see them, I'm not looking. I'm convinced that my defiance has become more discerning over time.

But the truth is that my alliances are what sustain and mobilize me now. I'm sustained by weekly Zoom-meals with my coworkers (our mission hasn't changed, but our priority has: taking care of ourselves). I'm sustained by the complicity and the pact we've made with our children to understand that everyone has a part to play, an obligation to fulfill — which includes, beyond homework and chores, the tasks of loving each other, taking care of each other, and forgiving each other when we blow a gasket. I'm sustained by the commitment I share with my partner to navigate this whole corona-situation with diligence and good humor (getaways and cuddling will have to wait). I'm sustained by daily contact with my loved ones here, with my loved ones in Spain: with my mother, who has taught me that neither she nor I, in our respective confinements, has the right to cave in; with my siblings, in our near-daily check-ins; with my friends, whom I try to touch base with once in a while. One friend has gotten sick and is pulling through.

Hospitalizations have doubled and ICU transfers have tripled in the last 48 hours. The governor of California has just announced that the state will need at least 50,000 more hospital beds to confront the wave of infections in the coming weeks. Horror looms. We'll soon learn whether the confinement measures adopted by counties in the San Francisco Bay Area, the first of their kind in the US, are bearing fruit.

Sooner or later, I know I'll lose myself in the catastrophic vastness of coronavirus territory, in the anguish of covid-19. When this happens, I'll reach for this map of my body-territory so I can reconnect with the woman I was until March 2020, and with the person I want to be, both during the pandemic and after. And when it's all over, there's something I won't forget: for the earth to breathe again, we humans had to stop.

THREE MATCHMAKERS: PANDEMIC 2

As it happens, after nearly eight months — two hundred-plus days—of following protocols for the acquisition and ingress of foods and objects into the house; of adhering to our family's rules for human contact, work, and education; of practicing *love by disinfection*, the catastrophic immensity of coronavirus territory — the horror of covid-19 — barely reached our periphery.

During this time, I tried to ground myself in the strength of my body-territory. But it was all in vain: by the end of the fifth month, my resistance collapsed under the ruthless effect of emotions. First came boredom, then helplessness, followed by stupor and rage, culminating in the utter cave-in of my body-territory due to enraged helplessness (or helpless rage, depending on which way you look at it). These five ingredients formed a mist of emotions that drenched me with pain, knocking me out for three whole days. Seventy-two hours in which I carried out my duties like a sleepwalker. All of them: as a mother, partner, daughter, sister, friend, employee, neighbor…sleepwalking one and all. Until today, as I sit down to write once again. Because maybe, as I realized by revisiting my account from March, writing may be my last stand, *clinging tooth and nail to my backbone, holding me up.*

But I'm not writing this record because I want to talk about my tightrope-walking with the pandemic despair of the past eight months, intensified by other despairs (feminist, anti-racist), and by the swift descent of the US democracy toward fascism (with the complicity of a delusional president, various Republican senators utterly lacking in political dignity, and many sheep-like voters). Instead, I want to talk about a new relationship. For the past couple of months, there's been a new woman in my life, thanks to the labor undertaken by three well-known matchmakers: *pandemic, quarantine,* and *global warming*.

It all begins with the global standstill, which sets in sooner here than in other states when the San Francisco Bay Area counties issue their orders to shelter in place, and Governor Gavin Newsom issues his own order for all of California. Before the first month of quarantine is over, settled into our daily family protocols and routines of *love by disinfection*, I'm informed that the publishing house I work for will be dispensing with my services for four months, as part of the temporary restructuring plan designed to withstand the drastic drop in sales and muddle through to the end of the year.

The equity that forms the foundation of my relationship and everyday life undergoes a dramatic change, and the responsibilities almost instantly fall to my partner. The busier her days get, the emptier mine grow. In order to survive the pandemic, she must become an essential worker, while I become essentially unemployed and shut away. And it drives me crazy. As this inoccupation demands nothing of me but essential inactivity, the days drag on. It's as if time had turned to liquid, and in this calm, which may or may not precede a storm, I must learn to float.

When our kids' school goes online and neither they nor their teachers nor we have any idea what the hell we're doing, I float. When the daily infection count in the US hits thirty thousand, I float. When quarantined Spain bleeds music and applause from people's windows, I think of my mother, who's spent months without hugging anyone, and I float. When I learn that more than half of the country I live in won't put on a goddamned mask and there are governors who refuse to demand their use in the full knowledge that lives will be lost as a result, I float. When our delusional president spews nonsense, I float. The more my partner runs from work to the store, from the store to her mother's house and from there to the neighbors' house, and the less I do (essentially), I also float.

To float, you have to be absolutely convinced that your body will rest on the surface without piercing the body of water, just like it does on the bed you sleep in every night. Floating isn't easy, but it can become easy. You don't know it at first, of course. Because at first the body sinks over and over before it can float, and it's only with practice that you realize sinking isn't inevitable. Only when you can persuade every muscle in your body to surrender to inertia is floating possible. You need faith to float, and faith is something you have to practice day after day.

As the weeks pass, I run out of spaces to float inside the house, so I step out into the yard. That's where I rediscover my plants. I don't have many of them: the house plants survive as best they can, and sometimes I move them from one spot to another in search of the perfect corner, where they can finally feel welcome and blossom as they deserve. But it rarely works. My partner and I take a now-rare trip to the store together and buy two tomato plants and some daisy plants that I soon discover are actually chamomile, and I pot them all. We used to have a plum tree that perished — of sorrow, I swear, after a gardener pruned it down to the core — so we buy a small maple and plant that in its place. One day I call my mother on WhatsApp as I water the yard. She says her father always spoke to his plants, even sang to them; plants listen, she tells me, they sense your presence, they feel accompanied. I start to talk to them. And sing, too.

Inside the house, I rotate the plants again, and I discover that one has gone entirely bare except for a single leaf. I transplant it into a little flowerpot and set it on the windowsill by the sink. Most mornings as I wash the dishes, I call my mother (I can't imagine what this pandemic would do to me if it weren't for WhatsApp). We have long, memorable conversations, laughing and raging and occasionally shedding a tear or two. Some days she sings. The idea is that the plant will listen, thinking we're talking and singing to directly to it; we want it to feel supported, encouraged to thrive. And it works! The little stem starts to grow. Out of that stem grows another, then two or three more, and the branch thickens into a trunk, and the trunk becomes a palm tree. Someone on Twitter talks about reading *What a Plant Knows* and learning that plants are sensitive to touch. Finishing the dishes, I stroke the sharp tips of the palm tree, go out into the yard, and tell the tomato plants about covid and quarantine, how lucky we are to live in the sunny, temperate microclimate of the San Francisco Bay. I gently touch their leaves. The chamomile doesn't look great; it's starting to dry out. I hold out the phone so my mother can see.

"Honey, it's burning up!" she yelps from Spain, slightly horrified.

"I ruined it, Mamá," I sigh, long used to my plants' sudden deaths.

"Plants are resilient, sweetheart. See that tiny green leaf? There's still life in it. Go find some shade where it'll still get a few hours of sun and keep watering it, and you'll see. Don't stop watering it!"

I keep floating in the bubble of this home we've made together. A new member joins the fold: a coronapuppy. The dog we swore we'd never have. But quarantine has made us reconsider all sorts of old convictions, and this is one of them. In Spanish, I'd say we've had to *replantear* — raise again, propose again — such ideas. I consider the root of that verb, then Google it: *repetition or reiteration of the active transitive verb* plantear *(to trace, to propose a plan), from "plant," from the Latin "planta," which means "the part of the foot that touches the ground.*

I let my fingernails grow longer and they darken with dirt. I walk along the creek, wearing pants riddled by the dog's fangs, my t-shirt smeared with his slobber. I have scratches on my legs and forearms from playing with him, pruning the orange tree, working in the soil. I've never felt as close to the earth as I am now. For the first time in many years, my feet *touch the ground*, are *planted* on it, and they don't wander the way they do when I get lost in my writing, when I escape on the meandering paths I trace on the page, or which trace me. By doing all of this, I guess I hope to shake off some ties that are no longer serving me in the pandemic context: I'm trying to transplant myself. We play, the earth and me, me and the earth; we talk to each other, look at each other, dote on each other. It's like reuniting with an old love. With it, I float. But in a different way: my floating is no longer an escape, but an arrival. Close to the earth, I feel like sinking is no longer inevitable.

On the night of Sunday, August 16, I'm jolted awake by the sound of several explosions. I open my eyes and find the walls of my bedroom spattered with a strange, elusive, flickering glow. Thunder and lightning, it turns out. They should be joined by rain, but the hours pass and the water never comes. For about five hours, 2,500 cracks of lightning were counted without a single drop of water. Those 2,500 will be followed by another 12,000, causing a total of 370 fires in three days. Several of them will converge in the SCU Lighting Complex Fire, which will become the third most devastating fire in California history — and which will force us to pack our bags. For the first time in twenty-two years, we may have to evacuate.

With the San Francisco Bay surrounded by fire and smoke, the air grows unbreathable and we're driven indoors. Right in the middle of record-breaking summer temperatures, with no air conditioning and the doors and windows sealed tight, the landscape beyond our walls takes on a post-mortem hue. Past the panes, the table and chairs in the yard, the plants, the cars, the tiles are all blanketed in ash. The hills, which peer past the trees at the end of our street, are invisible from the window. The phenomenon is much like the fog that creeps over the pavement on so many mornings, but this time the cloud floats along during the day, it's made of ash, and it consists of toxic particles that have traveled here from the north, from the south, from the east. I fantasize about fleeing west in a sailboat, all the way to Hawaii, but I discard this reverie right away — first because we don't have a sailboat, and second because my ridiculous idea is just the nerves talking. I have no idea which way I'd even run. As the days wear on, the light takes on an orange, Mars-like tinge that distorts what remains real — and is slowly ceasing to be so. I'm completely disoriented. My feet have never been so far from the ground. Not knowing where to plant them, the sinking feels inevitable again. This time, the earth sinks with me.

My brief, intense romance with this earth has opened something inside me: channels of communication that must have been blocked for generations. Arteries connected to an ancestral past whose symbiotic relationship with our planet we've chosen to strike down in exchange for larger, more efficient, more immediate systems of agricultural, industrial, and digital production. Some necessary, some irrelevant and still appealing to the consumer who seeks new forms of entertainment, striving to fill the time on their hands. And on this all-too-human course, which is the search for and conquest of the new and unknown, we've forgotten that almost everything we needed was already there. Like chamomile to calm our nerves and soothe our upset stomachs, or concentrated oil of oregano for asthma and fevers, to which we could have turned during the pandemic. Or the intentional fires once set by California's indigenous peoples in controlling the flames and vegetation that fed both themselves and the animals they hunted later — methods that could have helped us mitigate the tragedy of this summer, when four percent of the California countryside went up in smoke.

Progress involves many kinds of regression, and one of them is global warming. As the earth cries out and balks against our insatiable appetite for discovery, domination, extraction, and consumption, I think about the alliances I'm forging, as a queer woman and mother, to live with dignity. And I start to realize that one of them, maybe even the most important of all, might be with the earth herself.

DEAR PERSON

I'm writing this in your hours of deepest slumber, which is when you need me least, and I'm doing so in the form of a letter I'll tuck under our pillow, so you can take your time reading it over coffee, with our dog curled up at your feet, the way you like, as the others sleep on. Because it's your own body that writes you these words, but without you: you'll notice that the handwriting is a little different, slightly more legible than usual. You know how our tremors vanish when you sleep. In any case, I'm glad this will be easier for you to decipher than your own penmanship. Mine, I mean. The point is, I'm writing tonight in celebration of us. I guess it would have been fitting to organize some kind of surprise party, but I realized right away that you would've caught on — you being you, the one who controls all the thoughts and ideas. So instead I'm writing as you navigate the third phase of sleep. According to what I've read online, I have about a twenty-minute window, so I'll try to be brief. I hope you won't take this exercise of writing behind your back as a betrayal, but as an earnest attempt to access the depths of your consciousness with a proposition that, I'm convinced, will change our life (and our death, for that matter). With any luck, you'll give us a chance and receive it with an open mind and heart. Here goes.

Dear person of mine, I believe that the best possible way to celebrate our fiftieth birthday is by stopping time. My proposition is that we hit pause. I know this concept is hardly revolutionary or new; we've done it before, you and I. The thing is, though, we've never approached it in the way I'm suggesting now.

Do you remember the trips back home after the weekends we spent in your father's little hometown? He loved driving at night, so your mother would spread out blankets and cushions in back for you and your siblings to sleep there. Demis Roussos sounded on the tape player and you could see the stars through the window. Once you got home, you'd pretend to be asleep so that your dad would carry you up to bed, as he did with your younger siblings. You're pretty sure that your mother could tell you were faking it, but she never said a word. Those moments — "We Shall Dance" by Demis Roussos, the starry sky, your sleeping siblings, your father's shoulder, your mother playing along — were the pauses of your childhood.

What do you think you were all doing whenever the five of you burst out laughing around the table as a visitor noticed the incredible ascent of the second hand on the wall clock, leaping from the half-hour to the hour mark, followed by an insane plummet from the hour to the half-hour, all without ever ceasing to mark the proper time? Haven't you ever wondered why you never got that clock fixed? Or why you didn't warn the visitor in question? Well, because you loved watching the look on their face shift from confusion to discovery. A new reaction with every visit, and the helpless laughter that followed, and then the whole collection of such moments, like your trips to the little town: stamps of unforgettable family communion.

Now you're creating your own code of laughter and accompaniment, with its own unique pauses and its own familiar stamps that your own children will remember in the same way. Speaking of laughter, how about what your partner did the day you fell apart in front of her for the first time? It happened a few years after you moved into the apartment, when you were still working together. You'd had a tough week, if memory serves: you were homesick for Spain, you were struggling to get your freelance translation business off the ground, and your father was sick. Not knowing what to do with the pain, the helplessness, the melancholy, you told your partner to take the car by herself, because you wanted to bike the twelve-kilometer distance, needed to let off steam. You were teetering on the edge and you knew it. You said goodbye, slung your backpack over your shoulder, put your helmet on, and went into the storage unit to get your bike. When you saw it had a punctured tire, your heart sank. I saw it with my own eyes (well, ours). You dashed up the stairs to the building with your head ablaze. You opened the door, flung the backpack onto the floor with all your strength, shouted *Not even a fucking bike ride! Not eeeeven a fuuuucking bike ride!* and burst into tears of rage, right there in the doorway. Your partner didn't say a word, just went into the living room. You imagined her by the stereo, but you had no idea what she was up to, because you'd decided to let yourself crash and burn in your own frustration.

Until the song "Gonna Fly Now" from the *Rocky* soundtrack came on and she wove her way over to you, boxing. She made you get up, led you into the living room, and started boxing with you. You boxed together, jumped around, danced. You cried and she smiled. You punched the air and leapt and danced until you couldn't take it anymore. And then, snuffling, you hugged her at last, she bumped her head against the helmet you hadn't noticed you were still wearing, and you started to laugh. In fact, you laughed for days at the thought of your partner boxing, and of the two of you (now that you'd picked up on the *Rocky* allusion) climbing the stairs of the Philadelphia art museum in boxing gloves, you with your bike helmet still buckled under your chin.

You see, dear person, nothing halts the corrosive course of time like a moment of contemplation, a true belly laugh, or a good cry — or any combination of the three. I know I'm not saying anything I haven't heard you say before, but what I'd like to tell you is how those moments affect me. Without getting too deep into it, because I don't have much time, you should know that laughter and contemplation exercised as a regular practice release dopamine and serotonin (which help fight depression and anxiety) and endorphins (the happiness hormone, some call it, although I know that phrase gets your goat; we could define it instead as the pain-soothing hormone). They also limit the production of cortisol (the stress-causing hormone). It's similar with crying: it releases oxytocin (also soothing), adrenaline, and cortisol (there's that stress again), and most of all, when it comes to tears of joy or rage or sorrow, endorphins (again).

I know I lose you whenever I get too technical, my dear; I can tell by the little birdies that start fluttering around your head. As you can see, I'm trying my best to draw on a sense of humor I don't actually have and just copy you, my only model for human behavior.

What I'm getting at is, what if, instead of throwing the party of all parties to celebrate our fiftieth birthday, we organized hundreds of little parties? You know I'll follow you wherever you go, darling. If you get the blues, we'll slow things down, make room for the sadness, and cry a bit. If you're exhausted, we'll take a nap. That said, what I do want to ask you for the very first time in our long and fruitful relationship is that you take me out to party more often!

I know we can't dance for hours like we used to do with the girls on the handball team, or when you went to concerts with the boyfriends of your youth or the girl you dated after that. We can't even play soccer, or handball, or go running every day, or set out on long hikes with your kids, or take overly long trips. But what you can do is conjure the moments when you really connected with what life, being alive, meant to you. The moments when you could swear you demolished time; the minutes or hours or days when you felt like your experience on earth had transformed from something linear into a spiral of energy, pleasure, beauty, love, accompaniment.

Some experiences are unrepeatable; I won't pretend otherwise. I know you can't relive the day when, after your intense years as a goalie, the coach had you play the field because half the team was injured and you found yourself stealing balls right and left, scoring one effortless goal after another. You couldn't have stopped even if you tried. You experienced several of those spiral-moments during your handball years, and several other pancake-flat ones you mistook for spirals, moments that sent you crashing you to the ground.

You know what I'm thinking, right? Yes! The US handball championship. You'd reached the semifinals after quite a good week; you'd worked wonders at the goal. What's more, as you were warming up before the semifinals, a player from another team (later you'd learn that she was the captain of the national team) had asked if you were a US citizen, because they needed goalies for the Sydney Olympics. There would be tryouts, she said, and they'd love it if you tried out. You'd planned to check in after the championship. You were euphoric as the game began. You weren't good enough or tall enough to be a top-tier handball goalie in Spain, but the US was short on talent and they didn't care you were five foot three. The opposing team had several ex-Olympic champions, all incredibly tall European women. One of the Scandinavian Amazons stole the ball, and as she cut across the field like a bullet train, you did what you'd done so many other times to miraculous success: you decided to intercept her. After all, you were practically an Olympic athlete and had no time for nonsense! You leapt as high as you could, arms and legs spread wide to cover any possible gap, and you crashed right into her at what felt like six-and-a-half feet in the air. The Scandinavian player smashed you like a fly and you heard something crunch. The referee called a penalty, but you didn't care: you'd kept her from scoring. When you stood up under the crossbar and the whistle blew, your left knee buckled and you fell again. The Scandinavians screamed goooooal and you limped to the bench in tears. That was the end of your Olympic dream — which didn't last more than an hour, if I'm not mistaken. There was no other possible ending for your attempt to take down a decorated athlete a full six inches taller than you: the infirmary. You thought you'd experienced a spiral moment when it actually couldn't have been flatter. You should have been more careful. Don't make that face, I'm not blaming you for our misfortune, but facts are facts, and that's what's left to posterity.

What I'm asking you now is to reconnect with the essence of all those spirals. It's true, you won't be able to relive the day you first discovered what it meant to love another woman — physically, I mean. You'd taken pleasure in other flesh, men's flesh, but they were all flat, one-dimensional pleasures, predictable, easy to categorize. Instruction-manual orgasms in which everything had worked according to plan. Until you met the woman who would change everything. Two decades later, you're still trying to describe what you have together. More importantly, it still amazes you. I want you to hold onto that idea. The spiral-moments are the ones that amaze you, and every body (like the one writing you these words) is intrinsically capable of wonder, of conjuring energy, pleasure, beauty, love, accompaniment. That's what I call a party!

Your eyes are twitching, dear. You'll need me soon; it's time to dream. But before I go, some congratulations are in order. Even in the middle of a pandemic, you've found ways of taking me out to party: by writing this manuscript, for example, and reading books, sustaining conversations along the way; by taking those long walks of yours, with your partner or the dog; by driving to the coast; by exchanging hugs, messages, and songs with your daughter, you at home, her at college for the first time; by peppering the long silences of your fifteen-year-old son with hugs and vibrant conversations and laughter; by calling Spain; by sharing the touch and hugs and kisses that are slowly making their way back. The proof of such festivities comes when all those hormones I told you about get fired up and I can tell you're amazed. But I want more, dear person of mine. I want more and I want you to want more. So what do you say? Let's paint the town red.

I'm off, but here's a huge hug for you. Sweet dreams to both of us,

Your Body

POETICS OF THE SPINE

Melancholy seeps in
while memory slumbers
to dazzle me into exhaustion
Melancholy is the friend I never should have slept with

When **you yell** something lights up
and something switches off
inside me

What lights up
will hurt you
what shuts off
will hurt me instead

The piercing **buzz**
muffled to the woman who sleeps beside me
rattles against the walls of the night
woodworm of reality

I toss and turn

The space between
what's possible
probable
inevitable
narrows

I accelerate

on the dangerous curves of the hours
I'm a
derail
m
en
t

I dropped the **music**
Or it left

Or I scared it away

Now it's just the noise
my *soledad*
and I

My body is
a terrifying cozy
house of errors
with stunning views
and not a single door

Beyond the frame of its enormous window you can visit
me see
speak
listen
smell
touch
and
even feel

But you'll never know what it's like to be inside

and I'll never know what it's like to leave

She and I
shipwrecked *from different seas*
returned to the beach of that first caress
the alphabet surrendered to
dusk of stunned bellies

We came from different ports
in English
in Spanish
in crumbs of Portuguese
From salt-corroded maps
to calligraph our skin
in a fourth language
made only for us

Facing the Pacific
and its heaving waves
uncertain currents
without a compass
nautical chart
or sailing manual
we weighed anchor

She and I
Legs entwined
to keep us from drowning
Without a compass
nautical chart
or sailing manual
Survivors
for 23 prides

I wanted to get a tattoo of a **rose**

Instead of drawing it
on my hip
I moved in with her

She nestled all the same
on the iliac crest

I pulse for her

Her permanence is different
because
she
isn't
made
of
ink

She bleeds
and passes

Like me

With my head on her chest
where everything is possible
we dreamt of home

When the baby girl came
tiny soft innocent joyous
I drew my ear close
to the wild beating of her little heart
and trembled

When the little boy came
tiny soft innocent joyous
I trembled again
at the sound of his wild heart

Ever since
I've been the woman who pretends
she's not afraid

I'm their **mother**

The **cough**
maps a genealogical line
from grandmother to grandson
passing through the mother

The cough speaks
if you know how to listen
It's a matter of deciphering
tone timbre duration intensity

The cough is
alarmist
or reassuring

The cough can't ever
be ignored

The cough organizes the days and nights
the months and years
It draws up its own calendar
out of fear
or the anticipation of fear

The cough is the family metronome

There's a **chemical memory** forged from the metal of waiting

From vital signs, tubes, and suction pumps at homes and in hospitals
From stomachs contorting when it's time to say goodbye
From balls and chains cast with the heat of the family that sleeps apart
From knock-out hammer blows when a mother's care is not enough

There's a chemical memory forged from the metal of so much waiting
And a militia body entrenching itself

The six senses entrench themselves in their keenness
Adrenaline entrenches itself in its support
The appetite entrenches itself in survival
The stockpiles of fear entrench themselves in their hideaway

There's a chemical memory forged from the hypervigilance of waiting

And it always comes back

Even when the danger's gone

In its reptilian creep
from liver to throat
the **bile**
seared me

Many times

I swallowed
for
the good
communal
well-being

Many times

I was consumed

Many times

Full of black bile
and sick of swallowing
I predicted a shipwreck
mine? the very last?

I tossed
all excess luggage overboard
Mostly
people
Dead weight

Now
on the smooth course
of the aborted sinking

I try
to find
a place to put
the rage

amassed
with so
much
swallowing

Violence
like death

is a threshold
we cross **alone**

A trembling **woman**
isn't a doubting woman
or a fearful woman
She's a trembling woman

A tired woman
isn't a listless woman
She's a tired woman

A dizzy woman
isn't a weak woman
She's a dizzy woman

A woman with migraines
isn't a hysterical woman
She's a woman with migraines

A depressed woman
isn't a sunken woman
She's a depressed woman

A woman
isn't
your reading of her body
and its manifestations

In the restorative midday pause
I'm startled by the crunch
of my own **skin**

It speaks to me in cracks

It says it isn't easy
to be the wrapper
of a woman

That shedding emotions
is consuming

That age
is merciless

It says that in the next life
we'd be better off as onions

We'd have infinite skins
it adds

We are an onion
I reassure it

And get up to make myself some coffee

I have Jupiter
in the twelfth house
which protects me from the adversity
I'm not exempt from

Joy and optimism
live there too

Maybe
sustenance
is also in the **stars**

I’m **free** in the water
like when I make love with my partner
like in the first amniotic waters I dove into
that first freedom
before the existence of the rest of the world
where I never learned to be

The **words**
were the last to arrive
and will be the first to go

I normalize the impact of forgetting

I prepare for the formation of that gaping void beyond the tongue
where the syllables play for now
before they go out for a walk

I had
a 0.001%
chance
of winning the lottery

0.01%
of meeting my partner

3.5%
of being queer

10%
of giving birth by C-section

50%
of inheriting the tremor gene

I got it all

Fortune doesn't know a thing about math

As of tomorrow
I'll have lived longer in the US
than in my **country**

Weary of carrying
my body
asks me if
Spain
would weigh less

Not less
just different

That's what they say
and that's what I tell it
on this equidistant day of
February 13, 2022

I spilled **ink**
onto a body

to be read
in these pages

LOG OF WATERSHEDS

- A room at the San Ramón Clinic in Madrid, in 1970
- A mother and a father
- A US passport
- A sister
- A brother
- A runaway horse
- A round *mesa camilla* table
- A soccer ball
- Assorted insults
- A typewriter
- An intelligent and thoroughly non-condscending social science teacher
- A road trip around North America in a van
- A handball goal
- Menstruation
- A road trip around the other North America in a van
- A fainting fit, then another and another…

- A financial collapse following a betrayal
- An emotional collapse, maybe two, possibly three
- A migraine, then another and another…
- A book by Oriana Fallaci
- Another *mesa camilla* able, this one big enough to fit more people, more stories, more laughter
- A teacher besotted with language and literature
- Too much gin to keep track off
- A boy's smile, then another, another, another, another, another and another
- Also too much pain
- Endless laughter
- The mother who persisted
- The father who didn't know how
- A handball coach and his commandments from Rabindranath Tagore
- An unheated school and a protest
- A skiing trip that one of us never came back from
- An Interrail pass, then another
- A beating
- A narcissistic professor infested with misogyny
- A fit of vertigo, then another and another…
- A demonstration

- A news agency
- A warehouse
- A factory
- A call center
- One pending college credit
- A one-way ticket
- The semi-finals of the US handball championships
- Knee surgery
- A woman's collarbone
- A second language and a thousand misunderstandings
- A partner, the one with the collarbone
- An ICU and the funeral of the one who didn't know how
- An umbilical cord wrapped around a head and a C-section
- A daughter
- A son
- Another ICU, pediatric this time
- A corner of a hallway
- A ballot proposition to make us disappear
- A tremor, then another, another, another…
- A Torres goal
- Knee surgery again

- Misogyny and white supremacy in the *White* House
- Another demonstration, by women this time
- A novel, mine
- A pandemic
- A coronapuppy
- Another demonstration where our daughter is the one to raise her fist
- A shed of one's own
- A caretaker sister
- A caretaker brother
- A mother resisting
- Children, or really an entire generation, with nothing to lose
- A life with that partner, tending and resisting
- This manuscript, testimony of a body in resistance, my own

METADATA OF SUSTENANCE

attachments attachments attachments attachments attachments attachments attachments attachments attachments attachments attachments attachments attachments attachments attachments autonomy autonomy autonomy autonomy autonomy autonomy autonomy autonomy autonomy autonomy autonomy autonomy beginnings beginnings beginnings beginnings beginnings beginnings beginnings dependency dependency dependency dependency dependency dependency dependency dependency dependency dependency desire desire desire desire desire desire desire desire desire endings endings endings endings endings endings menstruation menstruation menstruation menstruation motherhood motherhood motherhood motherhood motherhood motherhood motherhood motherhood motherhood motherhood motherhood motherhood motherhood motherhood pain pain pain pain pain pain pain pain pain pain pain pain pain pain pain pain pain reproduction reproduction reproduction reproduction reproduction reproduction accident accident accident blood blood blood blood blood cry cry cry cry cry discrimination discrimination discrimination discrimination discrimination discrimination discrimination discrimination discrimination dissidence dissidence dissidence dissidence

dissidence dissidence dissidence dissidence emotionallabor emotionallabor emotionallabor emotionallabor emotionallabor emotionallabor emotionallabor emotionallabor emotionallabor emotionallabor emotionallabor emotionallabor emotionallabor emotionallabor emotionallabor expulsion expulsion expulsion expulsion expulsion expulsion expulsion expulsion expulsion fear fear fear fear fear fear fear fear fear fear fear fear fracture fracture fracture fracture fracture fracture fracture fracture fracture fracture infection infection infection penalization penalization penalization penalization penalization penalization penalization penalization rage rage rage rage rage rage rage rage rebellion rebellion rebellion rebellion rebellion rebellion struggle struggle struggle struggle struggle struggle struggle struggle struggle struggle struggle struggle struggle subjugation subjugation subjugation subjugation subjugation subjugation subjugation subjugation subjugation subjugation subjugation subjugation suffering suffering suffering suffering suffering suffering suffering suffering suffering suffering suffering illness illness illness illness illness illness illness illness illness illness illness illness resume resume standstill standstill standstill standstill standstill standstill standstill standstill vindication vindication vindication vindication vindication vindication vindication vindication vindication listening listening listening listening listening listening listening listening listening listening listening listening listening listening listening listening negotiation negotiation negotiation negotiation negotiation negotiation pact pact pact pact pact peoples peoples peoples care care care care care care care care care care celebration celebration celebration celebration celebration celebration dignity dignity

dignity dignity dignity dignity dignity dignity laughter laughter laughter laughter laughter laughter mobilization mobilization mobilization mobilization network network network network network rest rest rest rest rest alliance alliance alliance alliance alliance alliance equality equality equality equality education education education education education education habitat habitat justice justice justice justice justice manifesto manifesto manifesto manifesto manifesto manifesto manifesto noiseandsilence noiseandsilence noiseandsilence noiseandsilence noiseandsilence noiseandsilence readingandwriting readingandwriting readingandwriting readingandwriting readingandwriting readingandwriting readingandwriting readingandwriting reading and writing readingandwriting language language language language language language language language

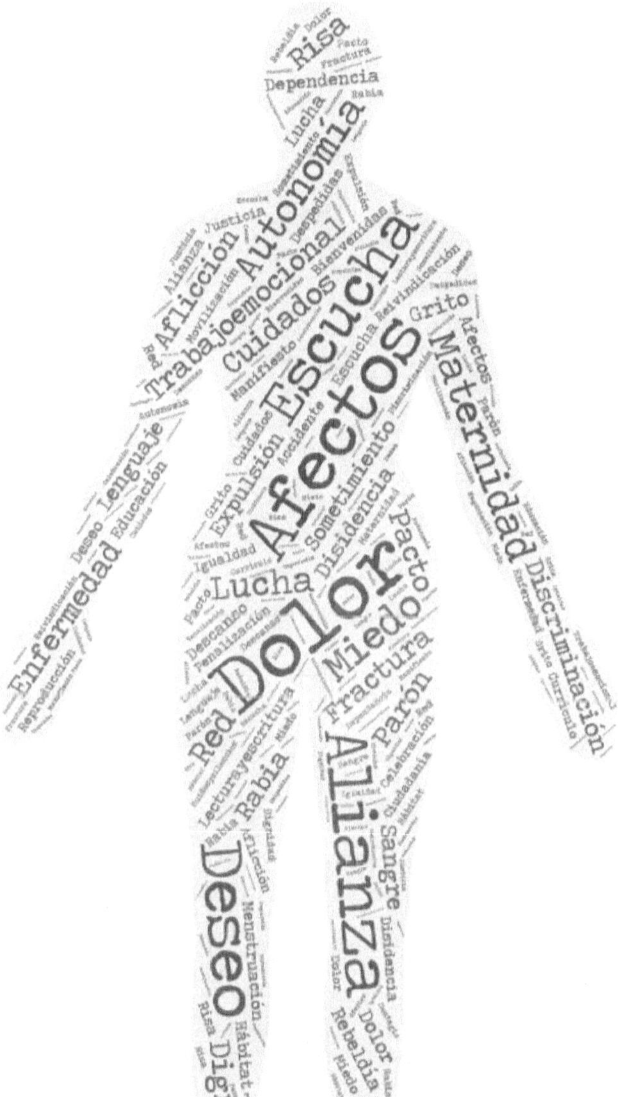

Risa
Dependencia
Lucha
Autonomía
Escucha
Afectos
Dolor
Alianza
Deseo
Dignidad
Negociación
Rebeldía
Maternidad
Discriminación
Currículo
Enfermedad
Lenguaje
Educación
Reproducción
Aflicción
Trabajoemocional
Cuidados
Justicia
Alianza
Bienvenidas
Despedidas
Expulsión
Grito
Sometimiento
Disidencia
Pacto
Miedo
Fractura
Parón
Red
Rabia
Lecturayescritura
Menstruación
Hábitat
Sangre
Celebración
Ciudadanía
Igualdad
Descanso
Penalización
Manifiesto
Reivindicación
Accidente
Contagio

EPILOGUE

I learned about totems — the creatures that represent us, our spirit animals — from one of my high school teachers. I'd heard the term some years back, on a road trip with my family, when I saw the eponymous wooden sculptures across indigenous land in northwestern North America. What I couldn't have imagined was the possibility of having my own totem.

At school that day, when I learned that mine was the dog and its best qualities were loyalty and nobility, I felt a sense of great excitement. Loyalty and honesty have always been important to me, which is why I never doubted being a dog. I questioned nothing about my spirit animal, not even its gender.

I was always proud of being a dog and loved behaving like one. Until three years ago, when this collection of texts started taking shape in my head and I went back to studying my spirit animal. That's how I found out that mine isn't actually the dog, but the wolf. This time I had no problem questioning its gender, taking on my true spirit animal (the she-wolf), and shouldering and celebrating everything it entails.

Why did 17-year-old María let herself be assigned "el perro" as a spirit animal, when the correct term would have been "la perra"? Why, on the cusp of my 15th birthday, did I see myself so clearly in the she-wolf, not the wolf?

While this anecdote isn't the origin of my book, it offers a metaphor for its raison d'être. It became a starting point for *Naming the Body* as I sought to reconstruct usurped language and identity. I gave voice to a body (mine, the only one I know) in order to explore its relationship with the person who inhabits it and the world it inhabits. I gathered its testimony, in all its voices and from all angles, to make it visible and do it justice — not as the powerful totem it contains, but as the magnificent, haphazard set of skin and bone and blood and neurotransmitters and antibodies it is.

Throughout this reconstruction, I also gradually discovered what sustains it; what sustains us both. What lets us see beyond our nearly fifty-two years on earth. In writing this book, I wanted to draw a map of the body, but the result goes further: it's a diagram for the future. Our future. My body's and my own. Your body's and your own. All of our bodies. Take up what's useful to you and make it yours. The rest will be nothing but a body's memory.

APPENDIX: THE #50HASHTAGS

CYCLE

attachments

autonomy

beginnings

dependency

desire

endings

motherhood

menstruation

reproduction

pain

RUPTURE

accident

blood

cry

discrimination

dissidence

emotional labor

expulsion

fear

fracture

infection

penalization

rage
rebellion
struggle
subjugation
suffering

PROTEST
illness
resume
vindication
standstill

AGREEMENT
listening
negotiation
pact
peoples

RECOVERY
care
celebration
dignity
laughter
mobilization
network
rest

VISION

alliance

equality

education

habitat

justice

manifesto

noiseandsilence

readingandwriting

AND MOST OF ALL

language

ACKNOWLEDGMENTS

In order for me to transfer this collection of texts from my head, heart, and guts onto the printed and digital page, it took many people, many conversations, many podcasts, lots of music, lots of books, many walks, and, of course, lots of writing. Here are just a few of them: thanks to my editor Maya Piña of El BeiS-mAn PrESs (US) and my editors Helle Bruun, Connie Dagas, and Mili Hernández of Editorial Egales (Spain), for giving me the time and space I needed to bring the #50hashtags into a book and thus to name the body.

Thanks to Anjanette Delgado and Sandra Lorenzano for their beautiful, incisive prologues to the Spanish-language editions. Thanks to authors Sylvia Aguilar Zéleny, Mila Martínez, and Norma Elia Cantú for their insightful readings and for their words of praise on the back covers. Thanks for my writing companions, Kris Malone Grossman, Verónica Llaca, Keila Vall de la Ville, and Maya Piña for the long conversations that accompanied the manuscript as it developed. Thanks to my boss, the editor Joan Pinkvoss, for our brief but intense chats about writing and publishing, stolen throughout our brutal hours at the office on pandemic Wednesdays, and for leading me to Gloria Anzaldúa.

Thanks to the writing residency Under the Volcano and to Sandra Lorenzano's workshop on writing and testimony. "This is a space of freedom," is how she opened the first session. And it was. Thanks to Sandra and my fellow workshop participants Gina Rodríguez, Oscar Molina, Patricia Carrillo Collard, Ramón Blanco, and Sofia Cerda Campero for their generous readings and comments, but especially for their writing. Thanks to Latin American, queer, and women writers of color for showing me the way. Thanks to Cristina Rivera Garza for *The Restless Dead: Necrowriting and Disappropriation*, a formative book and continual teacher for me. Thanks again to Sandra Lorenzano and her poetry, from which, by the way, I stole a few lines (see "*shipwrecked…*" in "Poetics of the Spine"). Thanks to Leonor Sánchez Martín for her reading, edits, and wise recommendations. I am grateful to Robin Myers' translation and the seamless way in which she captured the narrator's voice; and to Mouthfeel Press' Editor and Founder María Miranda Maloney for giving this collection a home and making it available to a whole new readership, this time in English. In a country where only three percent of published books are literature in translation, this is no small feat. Thanks to authors Anne Raeff, Kianny N. Antigua, Mariana Graciano, and Kadiri Vaquer Fernández for their generous reading and kind words on the back cover of this edition.

Thanks to the mother who resisted, and who accompanied the writing of this book with affection and clarifying questions and observations. She taught me so much, especially how to believe in myself. Thanks to my brother and sister for reading and believing, too. Papá, this text would have shaken you up, but you would have loved it. You always believed in women, and I wish you hadn't missed what we're making possible in this early part of the twentieth first century. Most of all, thanks to Rosie for sustaining me, sustaining us. Without you, love, writing wouldn't be possible. Thanks to Anna and Ian, to the three of you: for being, for being here, for loving, for accompanying, for believing. I love you, familia.

ABOUT

María Mínguez Arias is a fiction and non-fiction bilingual writer, accidental editor, translator, and journalist born in Spain and residing in California for the past three decades. She is the author of *Nombrar el cuerpo* (2022) named among the Best Queer Lit of the year in Spain, the Int'l Latino Book Award winning novel *Patricia sigue aquí* (2018), and co-editor of *#NiLocasNiSolas: narrativa escrita por mujeres en Estados Unidos* (2023). Her essays, short stories and reviews appear in anthologies and journals in the US, Spain, and Mexico. She delves into her identity as an immigrant, queer woman, mother, and Spanish-language writer in the US to explore subjects such as memory (digital, familial, and historical), motherhood, language, the body, and everyday life and strength as experienced on the margins. She is part of what has been coined the #NewLatinoBoom: a 21st century movement of writers, editors, publishers, and other literary professionals that, aided by all things digital, are collaborating in doing the work in Spanish and in the United States. She works as Co-Director of feminist press Aunt Lute Books in the San Francisco Bay Area, where she lives with her partner and their two young adult kids.

www.ingramcontent.com/pod-product-compliance
Lightning Source LLC
Chambersburg PA
CBHW030932060726
47591CB00005B/1760
9781957840505